Sugar-Free Cooking With

STEVIA

Sugar-Free Cooking With

STEVIA

The Naturally Sweet & Calorie-Free Herb

2ND EDITION

James & Tanya Kirkland

Crystal Health Publishing

First printing 1998

second printing 1998

third printing 1999, 2nd edition, revised

ISBN: 1-928906-11-7

Printed in the United States of America

Published by:
Crystal Health Publications
PO Box 171683
Arlington, Texas 76003-1683

Design, Layout and Typesetting by:
Studio 2D, Champaign, Illinois

Copy Editing by:
Margaret Shannon Stocks @ The Write Stuff

Recipe Editing by:
Lynda Karr

We dedicate this book to our daughters,
Tatiana and Sophia.
May your lives always be sweet!

Table of Contents

Introduction

Would you like to be able to sweeten foods and beverages without unwanted sugars and calories? Then stevia is for you. In late 1988, I encountered stevia - an incredibly sweet herb **with no sugars or calories**. The whole leaf form of stevia is about 15 times sweeter than regular refined sugar.

Back in 1988, stevia was available only in dried, whole or powdered leaf form and had a rather limited number of uses. Plus, whole leaf stevia can have a licorice taste - a turnoff for me. I found the whole leaf forms of stevia inconvenient and difficult to use. So, I continued consuming foods and beverages full of processed sugars and even worse, artificial (chemical) sweeteners. Finally, almost 10 years wiser (and a bit heavier), I decided to investigate stevia again. This is when I discovered Stevioside - the molecule that makes the leaves of the stevia plant sweet (more on this in Chapter 2). Standardized Stevioside is extremely sweet and a little bit goes a long way.

In 1996, I met a new type of stevia called stevia blend or spoonable stevia. This new form of stevia combines the stevioside extract with a non-sweet filler called maltodextrin to add bulk for easier measuring. With this wonder stevia, the herb can replace sugar in most recipes and beverages. Replacing sugary foods with stevia-sweetened foods allowed me to lose 20 pounds. This success inspired me to start work on the original *Cooking With Stevia*. I had no idea that the book would become a best-selling stevia cookbook or that it would even be temporarily **banned by the FDA** (more on this in Chapter 4).

There are over 200 recipes in this cookbook - favorites that have been kitchen tested and enjoyed by both children and adults. I hope that you and your family enjoy them as much as we do.

CHAPTER 1

Frequently Asked Questions

FAQ: FREQUENTLY ASKED QUESTIONS

1. What is stevia?

2. Is stevia safe?

3. Does stevia have any negative side effects?

4. What are the benefits of using stevia?

5. I have Candidiasis. Will stevia help this problem?

6. Does stevia have any effect on hypoglycemia or diabetes?

7. Can stevia help me stop craving sugar?

8. Where is stevia grown?

9. What are the types or forms of stevia?

10. Will stevia perform like sugar when cooking? Can I substitute it for sugar cup for cup?

11. Will stevia lose its sweetness at high temperatures like aspartame?

12. If stevia has been around so long, why am I just now hearing about it?

13. Why are stevia extracts so expensive?

14. Why aren't diet soft drinks sweetened with stevia?

15. What should I look for when purchasing stevioside or stevia blends?

What Everyone Should Know About Stevia:

1. What is stevia?

Stevia (pronounced steh-via) is a leafy green plant in the Asteraceae family, genus Stevia, species rebaudiana. Stevia is related to lettuce, marigold and chicory. You may be familiar with stevia by one of its many other names: Sweet Leaf, Caa-he-é, Erva Doce, and others. Dr. Moises Santiago Bertoni was credited with its discovery in the late 1800's. He named the plant *Stevia Rebuadiani Bertoni* in honor of a Paraguayan chemist named Rebaudi. The Guarani Indians in South America had been using the leaves of the plant to sweeten bitter teas and as a sweet treat for centuries. When Dr. Bertoni was given samples of the plant, he wrote "one small piece of the leaf will keep the mouth sweet for an hour."

2. Is stevia safe?

Stevia has been used since pre-Columbian times with no reports of ill effects. Stevia has also undergone years of research that have proven it safe for human and animal consumption.

3. Does stevia have any negative side effects?

Toxic? – No. Stevia has been used in Japan since 1970 and there have been no reports of toxicity or other side effects.

Mutagenic? – No. The Japanese Food and Drug Safety Center has found that stevia does not cause mutations of any kind. Only one study has shown stevia to be a potential mutagenic and this study was criticized for errors in procedure. Scientists in Great Britain reported that, according to the study's formula, distilled water would be considered a mutagenic.

A contraceptive? – Multiple studies have shown that stevia has no contraceptive effect. However, two studies have shown that stevia may have a contraceptive effect. The first of these was conducted in Uruguay over 30 years ago. Since then, no one has been able to reproduce the same results. A graduate student in Rio de Janeiro did a second study where his results and methods have been questioned.

Is stevia safe? – Absolutely. Stevia has been used around the world with no reports of overdose or toxicity to humans in the past forty years.

4. What are the benefits of using stevia?

While these benefits have not been approved or confirmed by the FDA, studies have shown that stevia has the following advantages:

- Sugarless & adds no calories

- 100% natural

- 250 to 300 times sweeter than table sugar

- Stable to 392° Fahrenheit (200° Celsius)

- Non-fermentable

- Flavor enhancement

- Plaque retardant – anti-caries (prevents cavities)

- Does not impact blood sugar levels

- Non-toxic

- Extensively tested and used by millions with no adverse effects.

5. I have Candidiasis. Will using stevia help this problem?

Candidiasis is a fungal yeast overgrowth in the body. This internal yeast thrives on sugar. Remove sugar and you remove its food source. Stevia will not promote fungal growth as it is a sugar-free natural sweetener.

6. Does stevia have any effect on hypoglycemia or diabetes?

According to the report, *Effect of the Stevioside and of the aqueous extract of Stevia Rebaudiana (BERT) Bertoni on the glycemia of normal and diabetic rats* (Professor Carlos Eduardo Pinheiro), Presented to the II Brazilian Convention on Stevia rebaudiana (Bert) Bertoni in September, 1982, it was found that the use of stevia did not produce any significant glycemic effects in normal or diabetic rats. In other words: stevia does not impact blood sugar levels. It allows the body to regulate blood sugar levels naturally. Of course, if you drink tea with stevia and eat a Twinkie®, all bets are off. Fortunately, if you take care with your diet, stevia is a wonderful way to satisfy cravings for sweets without added sugars. If you suffer from any type of blood sugar condition, please consult with your physician before using stevia.

7. Can stevia help me stop craving sugar?

Many people report that using stevia has helped them reduce or completely eliminate their sugar cravings.

8. Where is stevia grown?

Originally, stevia grew wild in the region of Northern Paraguay and Southern Brazil. Today, stevia is grown and used around the world from China, Japan and other Asian countries to South America, Europe, India, the Ukraine and even North America.

9. What are the types or forms of stevia?
(Also, see Chapter 2 – Types of Stevia)

Stevia Leaves

Fresh Leaves – Strong liquorice flavor. Fresh leaves contain 5–12% sweet glycoside: 4–11% Steviosides and 1–2% Rebaudiosides.

Dried Leaves – Dried form of the fresh leaves. Usually about 10–15 times sweeter than sugar. Used in brewing herbal teas and for making liquid extracts.

Tea Cut Leaves – Cut into small pieces and sifted to remove twigs and other unwanted matter.

Ground Leaves (Powder) - The dried leaves ground into a fine powder. Used in teas and cooking but does not dissolve.

Liquid Extracts

Dark – A concentrated syrup made from the dried leaves in a base of water and alcohol. Sweetness may vary between manufacturers. This form will offer the greatest amount of benefits from the stevia plant.

Clear – A solution of powdered steviosides dissolved in water, alcohol or glycerin. Sweetness varies between manufacturers.

Stevioside Powdered Extracts

80–100% Sweet Glycosides - The purified or processed form of stevia. The sweet glycosides are concentrated by removing unwanted plant matter. This off-white powder is 200 to 300 times sweeter than sugar. Quality of the powder depends on purity of the glycosides (i.e. 80–100% pure) and the ratio of rebaudioside A to stevioside. The higher the ratio, the better the product. Commonly referred to as "stevioside" or "white-powdered stevia."

Stevia Blends – Due to the great strength of the Stevioside Powdered Extracts, manufactures often add filler to "tone" down the strength. This makes the Stevioside easier to use and more palatable. These fillers are usually non-sweet food additives with little to no nutritive value such as lactose or maltodextrin. These fillers allow for easier measuring as well.

10. Will stevia perform like sugar when cooking? Can I substitute it for sugar cup for cup?

No. The molecular structures of sucrose (sugar) and stevioside are different. Sucrose, when heated, will brown or caramelize making such delights as gooey cookies, fudge and caramel possible. Stevia will not caramelize. In addition, you can not substitute stevia for sugar cup to cup. Because of these differences, cooking with stevia takes some practice. (See Successfully Cooking With Stevia.)

11. Will stevia lose its sweetness at high temperatures like aspartame?

No! The fact that stevia is heat stable is one of its best properties. Stevia is heat stable to about 392° Fahrenheit, or 200° Celsius, so it can be used in almost any recipe.

12. If stevia has been around so long, why am I just now hearing about it?

Stevia has been around for a long time, even in the United States. Early studies on stevia go back to the 1950s. In the '50s, the sugar industry fought to prevent the use of stevia in the United States. Greed, corruption and good old-fashioned politics have also stood in the way. Today, the manufacturers of the chemical sweeteners have lobbied the FDA to prevent stevia's approval as a food additive even though it is a new and better sugar substitute. If you have doubts, or want more information, contact "60 Minutes" at CBS. In the Spring of 1997, they aired a report on how the manufacturers of aspartame bought influence with the FDA to push the approval of a sweetener that is now blamed for many illnesses and deaths in America.

13. Why are stevia extracts so expensive?

There are actually many reasons. Stevia is a plant that has to be cultivated before it can be harvested for use as a sweetener. This requires large investments of capital to buy plants, farms, equipment, etc., to grow and harvest the plants. Then, there is the expense of processing the leaves into pure stevioside. When compared to sugar and the artificial sweeteners, yes, it is expensive because it is not as widely grown as sugarcane. Hopefully, with more countries growing and processing stevia, prices will soon fall. As for the more familiar chemical sweeteners, they are nothing but a blend of cheap chemicals. That is why these companies are so profitable. Due to the newness of stevia to the worldwide markets, inefficiencies and inflated expenses abound in the supply chain.

14. Why aren't diet soft drinks sweetened with stevia?

The answer is simple: Money! The diet soft drink market is huge – worth billions of dollars – and the manufacturer of aspartame is not about to share that market. Armies of lobbyists have been called in to make certain that the FDA did not approve stevia for use as a food ingredient. A patent on aspartame guarantees big profits – stevia is just a natural plant that can be grown by anyone and everyone.

15. What should I look for when purchasing stevioside or stevia blends?

1. A high rebaudioside to stevioside ratio. (Companies may not have this information.)

2. A high purity percentage, preferably over 90% steviosides. (100% stevia is not the same as 100% steviosides.)

    When purchasing pure stevioside try to find one that is un-bleached. It should be a creamy beige color.

3. Always buy from a reputable company.

CHAPTER 2

All Stevias Are NOT Equal

The Many Types of Stevia

Stevia is sold and used in more types than any other kitchen herb. It can be found in so many different forms that consumers are sometimes bewildered by their choices. Hopefully, this chapter will clear up any confusion about the various kinds of stevia, how they are made and their many possible uses.

Fresh Leaves

A fresh leaf picked or cut from a stevia plant is the simplest form of the herb. You can use the freshly picked leaves, or make a sweetening extract from them, in sauces and other similar foods. However, fresh leaves have limited uses – cupcakes or puddings can be difficult.

Herbal and other teas bring out the rich flavor of fresh stevia leaves. Steep them with your favorite tea blend or just on their own for a wonderful sugar and chemical-free beverage. Stevia does have a unique flavor - most people describe the natural taste of stevia as a mild licorice flavor. Keep in mind that refined sugar is processed until its natural flavor is gone. Chemical sweeteners (aspartame, saccharin, etc.) are designed to be more palatable to consumers by imitating the taste, or lack thereof, of table sugar. You may have corn syrup, molasses, pure maple syrup or honey in your kitchen - good examples of natural sweeteners. Like stevia, each is sweet in its own way and has a distinct taste. However, they all add calories and/or sugars to food. Stevia allows you to sweeten food without adding calories, sugars or processed chemicals to your diet. For more information, see our web page at www.steviapetition.org.

Dried Stevia Leaves - very self-explanatory: fresh stevia leaves are dried to remove all water, allowing for longer storage periods. Traditionally, stevia leaves are harvested on a farm and allowed to dry under the hot summer sun. Dried stevia leaves have basically the same uses as fresh leaves.

Ground Stevia Leaves – Like most other herbs, stevia can be ground into powder. The basic idea, to use the ground leaves like sugar, has one problem - sugar dissolves in liquids, ground stevia does not. Finely ground stevia leaves can be used in the same manner as fresh or dried stevia leaves, but fall short when making a pie or cake. I remember making a vanilla pudding with ground leaves, once. The end result was a pasty green pudding that had more licorice taste than vanilla. Yes, you can cook with the ground leaves . . . but there are better stevia alternatives out there.

Stevia Liquid Extract (Stevia Syrup)

Stevia syrup may sound good but hold that thought. A dark, greenish-black liquid, it is 100 to 150 times sweeter than simple sugar syrup, not at all like maple or corn syrups. Remember that stevia has a slight licorice taste? Now imagine that mild flavor a 100 times stronger. The intense licorice taste can be very bitter – beware, this extract is extremely concentrated! In an 8 oz. glass of water, 3 to 10 drops (depending on the brand and concentration) should be sufficient to sweeten it. The end result is actually a glass of stevia tea, but when used in coffee, tea or other beverages, it works well.

How is stevia syrup made? Dried stevia leaves are re-hydrated with water, crushed or pressed to extract the liquid and the resulting solution is cooked down to make syrup. Some form of preservative is usually added to prevent spoilage. Some manufacturers use alcohol - sometimes as much as 18% alcohol or higher (that's 36 proof or as much as some liqueurs!). Other manufacturers use grapefruit seed extract or some other form of approved preservative.

Stevia Steviosides (also called "White Stevia Powder")

In the world of non-caloric sweeteners, if there were gold at the end of the rainbow, it would be called steviosides. Hidden deep within the leaves of the Stevia Rebaudiana plant, a group of molecules (glycosides) give the stevia plant its sweetness. The active components of these glycosides are molecules called steviosides. These steviosides make up about 5–15% of the plant. This molecule is intensely sweet - about 300 times sweeter than sugar. It has no fat, no calories, no processed sugars and no carbohydrates. It basically does nothing but taste sweet. The stevioside molecule has some close cousins, rebaudioside A, rebaudioside B, and others, which are even sweeter than the stevioside. Unfortunately, they exist within the stevia plants only in very small amounts, about 2–3%. When *any* of these molecules are extracted from the plant, they fall under the term "Steviosides." So when you read "Steviosides" on a label, it refers to all of the stevioside molecules (cousins included), not just the one stevioside molecule.

Quality

Quality can be addressed in four basic categories: ratio, purity, additives, and other.

Ratio: When dealing with stevioside, the "ratio" tells you how much of the steviosides is stevioside and how much is actually its cousin glycosides, such as rebaudioside A & B. Since the rebaudioside glycosides are much sweeter and have a much better taste (similar to fructose), you would think that everyone would want pure rebaudioside. An attractive idea but not very feasible. Rebaudioside A appears in very minuscule amounts (some stevia hybrids have slightly higher percentages than others) – so to extract pure rebaudioside A would not only be difficult, but cost prohibitive.

You want to look for a good ratio of rebaudiosides to steviosides when you purchase stevia. The higher the ratio, the better the product – if indicated on the label, a 90% ratio is a good one. Unfortunately, at this time, most stevioside distributors do not list the ratios and many do not even know the ratio of their product.

Purity: Purity refers to the percentage of steviosides (including the other glycosides), to all other components such as fiber, water, cellulose, chlorophyll, etc., and any other matter (including chemicals) that were used to process the steviosides. This other stuff can greatly affect the taste of the stevioside. Since I started using stevia back in the late 1980's, I have seen a range from a bitter 70% pure steviosides to a wonderful Japanese sample with over 98% steviosides. What made the Japanese sample even more delightful is that it also had a very high rebaudioside to stevioside ratio. This stevioside tasted like a super-sweet powdered sugar. Unfortunately, this source is no longer available and it was also very expensive at over $200 per kilogram.

Additives: I have recently seen some very disturbing trade practices when it comes to stevia. Stevioside has no need for added sweeteners. Unfortunately, some samples of steviosides from China and Korea contained stevioside, rebaudioside and an artificial sweetener such as aspartame, saccharin, and/or aculfame K. Some of the first samples that I received listed these chemicals as additives, probably to cover the poor quality of the steviosides; but lately, I've seen some samples that were just "too good." After having the samples tested, it was discovered that chemical sweeteners had been added – even though the final product was being marketed as **pure** stevioside. Why would anyone do this? Simple: GREED!

Stevioside can be very costly to make since the stevia plant has to be grown, harvested and then processed. There are various methods of extraction, using both chemicals and water. The latter is best and is a closely guarded trade secret within the industry to maintain competitive advantage. Chemical sweeteners are cheap to make and if no one has ready access to a lab, easy to hide.

To avoid these rip-offs, purchase stevia only from reputable companies with a history of dealing with the herb. Some companies are trying to get onto the "stevia bandwagon" and they may knowingly, or unknowingly, be selling adulterated (not 100% pure) stevioside.

Other: The extraction of stevioside from the stevia plant is a very tricky process. One that not many people (including me), fully understand. The best methods use as few added chemicals as possible. Although these more natural methods cost more, they do yield a far superior product. Other methods use a lot of chemicals. Some even bleach their product to make it white like table sugar. While these products may be attractive and look more familiar, they usually taste bitter.

All Stevias Are NOT Equal

Clear Liquid Stevia Extract

Manufactures dissolve the pure stevioside into water to create a product that is sweet, concentrated, attractive and most important, pleasant tasting.

Using liquid extract can get expensive rather quickly. Its best use is sweetening drinks like coffee, tea, milk or other favorites, where just a few drops will suffice.

Quality: The quality of the liquid depends on two factors: 1) the quality of the stevioside used to make the extract, and 2) what additives, such as preservatives, are used. As explained before, these preservatives can sometimes affect the taste and even the alcohol content.

Stevia Blends (also called "Spoonable Stevia")

Stevia blend is an important term in this cookbook. Be careful - it can mean the blending of steviosides with some form of chemical sweetener such as aspartame (which defeats the purpose of a natural sweetener). A good stevia blend is a high quality stevioside with a non-nutritive filler acting as a bulking agent. When consumers first used Saccharin, they complained that it was too sweet. So the manufacturers blended saccharin with a non-nutritive filler such as maltodextrin (derived from cornstarch with no real nutritive value and almost no sugar) which makes it easier to measure. Following this method, some makers of stevioside have begun to blend it with filler to make for more familiar measuring. What used to be 300 times sweeter than sugar is now only four times as sweet (a 4:1 stevia blend to sugar ratio). Although not an industry standard, this is the most widely used ratio.

Stevia blends are so easy to use – they will mainstream stevia as a sweetener for the future. Consumers are already accustomed to the 4:1 ratio used with saccharin, aspartame and other chemical sweeteners. There are many recipes for these chemical sweeteners that will easily convert for use with stevia blends. One caution: when using a recipe that calls for aspartame such as Equal" (which is aspartame and a filler), you might need to use less of the stevia blend. These recipes often use more aspartame than needed to compensate for the fact that aspartame breaks down with heat. Fortunately, stevia is heat stable up to 392° Fahrenheit.

Quality: The same criteria used for stevioside holds true in determining the quality for stevia blends.

Dietary caution

A quick note for those with special dietary needs: the most common filler in stevia blends is some form of maltodextrin. These fillers, while having little or no sugars, may still contain carbohydrates (but in a minuscule amount when compared to sugar). This is not a problem for most consumers, but it can be a great concern to diabetics and those who are on a very carbohydrate-restrictive diet. Please discuss your particular dietary needs with your doctor and/or nutritionist.

CHAPTER 3

Stevia, the FDA and the First Amendment

Why This Book Was Banned!

The Controversy and the Ban

Stevia has been used for centuries in South America and is the most popular non-caloric sweetener in Japan. In 1980, aspartame was approved for use as an artificial sweetener . . . around the same time that saccharin was pulled off the market after studies showed when rats consumed huge unrealistic portions that their was a potential cancer risks - coincidence? Stevia's own relationship with the Food and Drug Administration (FDA) is controversial at best. In the late 1980's, health food stores began selling stevia as a natural sugar substitute. When the FDA received an anonymous complaint about stevia, all imports and sales of the herb were banned in the US. After years of pressure from consumers and the health food industry, Congress passed the Dietary Supplement & Health Education Act in November 1994. This act permitted the purchase and sale of stevia as a dietary supplement - not as a food or food additive. The Act also set forth rigorous guidelines for the labeling, sales and marketing of the herb. Simply suggesting that the stevia be mixed with water could be construed as mislabeling and force a recall of the products. These burdensome regulations eventually led to the FDA's order to ban this book. For more information about the stevia/FDA controversy, read *The Stevia Story, A Tale Of Incredible Sweetness And Intrigue* by Linda & Bill Bonvie and Donna Gates.

The FDA Destruction Order

On May 19,1998, the president of Stevita Company (a distributor of Stevia in Arlington, Texas) received a fax from the Dallas District Office of the FDA - it ordered the seizure and destruction of *Cooking With Stevia* and other literature. The fax read: "...a current inventory must be taken by an investigator of this office, who will also be available to *witness destruction of the cookbooks*, literature, and other publications... Additionally, your stevia products currently in distributor and retail channels with the offending cookbooks, literature, and other publication continue to be in violation of the Federal Food, Drug, and Cosmetic Act. *These products are unapproved food additives* in violation of Section 409, and *adulterated* within the meaning of Section 402(a)(2)(c) of the Act." (Italics added for emphasis.)

What is the real reason these publications were singled out for destruction? Mary Nash Stoddard (founder Aspartame Consumer Safety Network) sums it up in an article she wrote in June of 1998:

"Do these books tell people how to commit terrorist acts? No. Do they contain pornography of *any* kind? No. Do they instruct potential criminals on how to set up a lab to produce LSD or Crack Cocaine: No. The FDA ordered the drastic action because the books contain general information that includes: history, usages and scientific studies regarding stevia – a naturally sweet non-caloric herb with an impeccable history of safe use – and because current federal law requires that stevia herbal products be marketed as dietary supplements without being labeled as sweeteners."

According to the FDA regulations, Stevita Company's sale of stevia-related publications was illegal. Allegedly, the FDA even raided local health food stores looking for my offensive cookbook. While/Although it is legal to sell literature about the stevia herb, but store owners may not place the publications *next to* the supplements. The FDA took this regulation a step further by implying that Stevita Company's distribution of Cooking With Stevia somehow violated the stringent labeling regulations imposed on stevia. Regulations like these continue to frustrate everyone in the health food industry.

Cooking With Stevia - Marked for Destruction by the FDA

That same day, two agents of the FDA arrived at Stevita Co. to inventory all of the company's stevia supplements, books and promotional literature. Then they met with the company president to discuss the recall and destruction order of Cooking with Stevia. Just as their conversation began, a crew from a local news station arrived. The mood changed quickly as the FDA agents questioned why the reporter was there.

The president's reply: "To record the burning of the books!"

FDA agents allegedly said: "Oh no, we are not going to burn the books, YOU are!"

President (after a brief pause): "I'm sorry, I can't do that. I don't have a permit from the local fire department. You'll have to do it."

The two agents whispered back and forth before deciding to call their office for further instructions. They were told to mark all of the remaining *Cooking with Stevia* books by initialing and dating the inside covers of each book. Supposedly, these marks would help keep track of the cookbooks until they were officially destroyed. In reality, once marked, these books were no longer 'new' and could not be sold in the stores. This action was taken by the FDA without a court order authorizing the destruction of private property.

As it ended up, my books were not officially destroyed that day. However, during the following months, the FDA seized all of Stevita's inventory – in an effort to force the company to comply with the recall and destruction order. This action practically put Stevita Company out of business. Only after lengthy litigation was the company allowed to resume distribution of some publications, but not *Cooking With Stevia*.

You Can Help

The authors of *The Stevia Story, A Tale Of Incredible Sweetness And Intrigue*, Linda and Bill Bonvie, posted the following on their internet website:

"Given stevia's record as a completely safe (and beneficial) herbal product, and given that it now may be purchased legally in the country, just what is the FDA afraid of? That Americans will learn about stevia – that it's actually both sweet and non-caloric? Try it? Want to use it? The FDA's prior attempts to control stevia as if it were a dangerous drug had the appearance to many of being a restraint of trade; now that it can be legally sold and used, the agency has gone further and is apparently trying to restrain ideas, information and criticism of its own behavior – trying, in essence, to act as a sort of 'thought police.' This is a very important issue, which should be carefully followed by everyone – whether you like stevia or not – even if you've never tasted it."

Go to our website: www.steviapetition.org and gather more information. Decide how you can get involved to stop the government from railroading this wonderful herb.

CHAPTER 4

Successful Cooking With Stevia

How To Kick The Sugar Habit

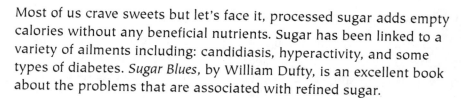

Most of us crave sweets but let's face it, processed sugar adds empty calories without any beneficial nutrients. Sugar has been linked to a variety of ailments including: candidiasis, hyperactivity, and some types of diabetes. *Sugar Blues*, by William Dufty, is an excellent book about the problems that are associated with refined sugar.

Step one to kicking the sugar habit is to replace processed sugar with nature's sweetener – stevia. You can substitute stevia in your favorite recipes by following a few simple tips. Since stevia extracts are so highly concentrated, just a little will go a long way - you can replace a whole cup of sugar with just a small amount of stevia. Be sure and follow our conversion charts carefully for the best results.

Tips For Cooking With Stevia

The first thing to remember is that stevia is sweet but not exactly like sugar. Comparing stevia to sugar is like comparing molasses to honey or maple syrup to corn syrup. All are sweet but each one has a unique taste, and, when properly used, can produce wonderful results in many types of recipes.

The next trick to using this herb is to understand how its sweetness differs from more common refined sugars. Start by purchasing a small alcohol-free bottle of the clear liquid stevia extract (see Types of Stevia in Chapter 2) from your local health food store. Add a few drops of the liquid to a glass of water. Taste it. It will be sweet without the refined sugars and chemicals found in processed sweeteners. Alternate between adding drops of clear liquid extract and tasting until the mixture becomes bitter-sweet. It is this bitter-sweetness that can sometimes make stevia difficult to work with - you will soon get the hang of using just a small amount.

Some people love the taste of stevia while others take a while to adjust to the mild liquorice taste. Here's a hint to help your taste buds forget about sugar: Try adding a little spreadable fruit, frozen white grape juice concentrate or even a little unrefined (or turbinado) sugar until your body adjusts to the natural sweetness of stevia. In just a short while, you should be able to phase into using stevia alone.

Cooking with stevia can have some limitations. Stevia does not brown or caramelize like sugar. Baked goods, especially cakes, may not rise as well. When using stevia, we lose the bulk that sugar adds to recipes. Achieving that "gooey – chewy" cookie texture takes a little practice, but is not difficult. Don't despair - in this book, you will find many secrets to successful cooking with stevia.

Secrets of Cooking With Stevia

Cookies: Always preheat the oven to the recommended temperature. Crisp, short-bread types of cookies give the best results. For softer, chewy cookies, add some canned pumpkin, uncooked oatmeal or even peanut butter. Never over-bake "soft" cookies - keep an eye on them in the oven. Another way to achieve a softer cookie texture is with bar or pan cookies like brownies. Their texture and thickness will help satisfy your chewy cookie cravings.

Cakes: Always preheat oven to the recommended temperature. The secret to moist and light cakes is whipping the eggs to super-stiff peaks (try separating the whites and beating them first) then folding in the dry ingredients, similar to making an angel food cake. After removing the cooked cake from the oven, immediately invert the pan onto a cooling rack. This prevents the cake from falling.

Flavorings and Extracts: Flavorings and extracts like maple, orange, and vanilla are great ways to mask the natural licorice flavor of stevia while adding depth and interest to your dish.

Dairy: Stevia extracts work great with milk, cream, cream cheese, sour cream and other dairy products. That is why we use dairy products in so many of our recipes.

If you are dairy or lactose-intolerant, I have had great success with replacing the milk with Almond Milk (see index), reconstituted powdered tofu such as Better Than Milk® or rice milk (both tofu milk and rice milk are available at health stores). These work well but can be high in sugars so read the labels carefully.

Beverages: This is the easiest place to use stevia. A few drops of clear liquid extract or a pre-measured packet will make any beverage taste better. Try some in iced or hot teas, coffee, lemonade, Kool-Aid®, and other beverages with traditionally high sugar content.

Breads: *Yeast Bread* – A common misconception is that yeast breads won't rise without a sugar to act as a catalyst. However, bread can rise with just the flour to feed the yeast – this process will take just a bit longer.

Quick Breads – As with cakes, stevia-sweetened quick breads tend not to rise as well as conventionally sweetened breads. We have made adjustments in the amounts of baking powder or soda in our recipes to give you amazingly delicious sugar-free muffins and breads.

Mixing: The final secret to successful cooking with this herb is to carefully blend the stevia extract with the other ingredients. Stevia blends (see Types of Stevia in Chapter 2) are easy to work with. However, pure stevioside is so concentrated that you must be careful not to use too much. We recommend thoroughly mixing stevioside with the dry ingredients before adding the wet ingredients or completely dissolving the stevioside one of the liquid ingredients. It's important that the stevia extract be thoroughly combined with all the other ingredients or your baked goods may not turn out as you expected.

CHAPTER 5

Beverages

BEVERAGES

Almond Milk – 40

Eggnog – 35

Hot Chocolate – 33

Hot Cocoa – 33

Hot Mocha – 33

Iced Cappuccino – 36

Instant Cocoa Mix – 34

Jungle Smoothie – 42

Kool-Aid® Punch – 37

Lemonade / Limeade – 37

Old Fashioned Root Beer (and other soda pops) – 38

Orange Jubilee – 41

Peachy Yogurt Shake – 42

Pineapple-Peach Smoothie – 43

Sparkling Punch – 40

Spiced Cider – 34

Spiced Hot Cocoa – 33

Stevia Fruit Smoothie – 43

Strawberry Fizz – 41

Hot Chocolate

2 squares (2 ounces) unsweetened coarsely chopped chocolate
4 teaspoons stevia blend *or* $1/2$ tsp. stevioside
4 cups milk
Whipped Cream (optional—see index)

In a medium saucepan, combine unsweetened chocolate, stevia, and $1/2$ cup of the milk. Cook, stirring constantly, over medium heat till mixture just comes to boiling. Stir in remaining milk; heat through. Do not boil or it could curdle. Remove from heat. Serve hot in cups or mugs. Top each serving with whipped cream, if desired.

Makes 4 servings.

Variations

Hot Mocha: Prepare as above, and stir 1 tablespoon instant coffee crystals into hot chocolate milk.

Spiced Hot Chocolate: Prepare as above, and stir $1/2$ teaspoon ground cinnamon and $1/4$ teaspoon ground nutmeg into chocolate milk.

Hot Cocoa: Prepare as above, substituting $1/4$ cup unsweetened cocoa powder for the chocolate.

Instant Cocoa Mix

2 cups nonfat dry milk powder
$1/2$ cup powdered nondairy
   creamer

$1/2$ cup unsweetened cocoa
   powder
5 teaspoons stevia blend *or*
   $5/8$ tsp. stevioside

For cocoa mix, stir together milk powder, nondairy creamer, cocoa powder, and stevia blend. Store in an airtight container.

For each serving put $1/3$ cup mix in heat-proof mug. Add $2/3$ cup boiling water. Mix well.

Variations

Mocha Mix: Prepare as directed, except reduce the cocoa powder to $1/3$ cup and add $1/4$ cup instant coffee crystals.

Spiced Cider

4 cups apple juice or apple cider
$1/2$ teaspoon cinnamon
$1/2$ teaspoon allspice
$1/4$ teaspoon ground cloves

1 teaspoon stevia blend *or*
   $1/8$ tsp. stevioside
4 each cinnamon sticks (optional)
4 each orange wedges (optional)

Mix all ingredients together in a large pot. Bring to boiling, stirring occasionally: reduce heat. Cover and simmer at least 10 minutes. Serve cider in mugs with cinnamon sticks or orange wedges, if desired.

Makes 4 servings.

Eggnog

6 each eggs
2 cups milk
1 cup whipping cream
1 teaspoon vanilla
3 teaspoons stevia blend *or*
   3/8 tsp. stevioside

Garnish:

Whipped Cream (optional, see index)
cocoa, ground nutmeg or cinnamon

In a large saucepan, mix eggs, milk, cream, and stevia blend. Cook over medium heat, stirring constantly, until mixture coats a metal spoon. Remove from heat. Cool quickly by placing pan in a sink of ice and continuing stirring for a few minutes. Add vanilla. Chill 4 to 24 hours. Top each serving with whipped cream, if desired, and sprinkle with choice of garnish.

Makes 4 servings.

Iced Cappuccino

**WITH A HINT OF ORANGE,
THIS IS TRULY A REFRESHING TREAT.**

7 1/2 cups cold water
1 teaspoon orange zest (optional)
1 1/2 cups drip grind espresso
   coffee
3 cups milk
3 to 4 teaspoons stevia blend *or*
   3/8 tsp. stevioside

Garnish:

Whipped Cream (see index)
cocoa, ground nutmeg or
   cinnamon

Place orange zest in bottom of coffee pot. Brew coffee using cold water
and espresso; cool to room temperature. Strain coffee and discard
orange zest; stir in stevia blend and milk. Refrigerate until chilled.

Pour cappuccino into glasses; spoon small dollops of whipped topping
on each and sprinkle with cocoa, nutmeg or cinnamon.

Makes 10 servings.

Beverages

Kool-Aid® Punch

1 packet Kool-Aid® brand or other unsweetened punch mix
3 teaspoons stevia blend *or* ³/₈ tsp. stevioside
2 quarts cold water

Empty packet contents into a large plastic or glass pitcher. Add stevia and mix well. Add cold water and ice to make two quarts and stir until dissolved. If having problem getting the stevioside or stevia blend to dissolve, place punch in refrigerator for ¹/₂ to 1 hour and then stir again. Serve cold.

Note: If you prefer sweeter Kool-Aid®, dissolve more stevia blend into the punch in ¹/₂-teaspoon increments until sweetened to taste.

Makes 8 servings.

Lemonade / Limeade

4 cups water
1 cup lemon juice or lime juice (4 to 5 medium lemons *or*
    7 to 10 medium limes)
2 teaspoons stevia blend *or* ¹/₄ tsp. stevita liquid
ice cubes

In a pitcher, combine water, lemon or lime juice, and stevia. Stir till stevia dissolves. Add more stevia in very small increments if you like it a little sweeter. Serve over ice or chill till serving time.

Makes 5 servings.

Old Fashioned Root Beer

AND OTHER SODA POPS

1 gallon water
$^{1}/_{2}$ tsp. stevioside *or* 4–5 tsp. stevia blend
1 tablespoon root beer extract (or other soda extract)
2 tablespoons sugar (to ferment yeast*)
$^{1}/_{4}$ teaspoon yeast

In a cup of warm water, dissolve yeast (you can use wine or beer yeast and even bread yeast but champagne yeast gives a better taste). Let stand for 5 minutes or longer to dissolve.

Combine extract with warm water, sugar, and stevioside. Stir well to dissolve sugar and stevioside. Add yeast mixture. You can taste the mixture to make adjustments to sweetness and flavor.

Sterilize bottles in boiling water. Gently pour mixture into each bottle until 1-2 inches from top. Cap each bottle with caps (follow manufacturer's instructions for preparing caps).

Place bottles in a warm area, 75 to 85° F, for 3 to 4 days. Check carbonation. If carbonation is satisfactory, place in refrigerator to stop carbonation process and to chill the drink. If carbonation is not yet satisfactory, allow to sit in a warm area for another day or two, check carbonation, and if okay, chill. When serving, try not to disturb the yeast that will have settled to the bottom of the bottle. Most people do not like that "yeasty" taste in their beverage.

Experimenting: Most soda pop flavorings can be purchased at any home brewing supply store. This will allow you to try different flavors and mix them. One favorite is cherry-cola, which is simply a mixture of the cola extract with the cherry extract.

Beverages

Caution: depending on the temperature, the carbonation process may be faster or slow; so be careful because the bottles could pop if it is too fast. Since the sugar content is low, the carbonation process is limited due to a lack of food for the yeast.

Makes 24 servings.

---

*If you are wondering why there is a need for sugar, the answer is simple. Carbonation is achieved when the yeast turns the sugar into alcohol and carbon dioxide. Fortunately, due to the low sugar content and the short carbonation period, the beverage will have virtually no alcohol and lots of bubbles. Also, the yeast will consume the sugar during the process of carbonating the water. Since stevia is not a sugar, the yeast will ignore it and when all of the sugar is consumed, the yeast will die off.

Sparkling Punch

1 liter carbonated water (seltzer water)
1 teaspoon stevia blend *or* ⅛ tsp. stevioside
½ package unsweetened Kool-Aid® type punch mix

Mix the stevia and punch mix into ⅛ cup of the carbonated water. Stir until dissolved. SLOWLY add this solution to the carbonated water. The carbonated water will foam up so watch it carefully, and go very slowly. Once all the stevia solution has been added to the carbonated water, seal the bottle very tightly, and carefully mix. Refrigerate until cold. Serve cold or over ice. Now you can make any flavor carbonated beverage that you can find as a Kool-Aid® type punch mix.

Makes 4 servings.

Almond Milk

4 cups water, ice cold
1 cup raw almonds
2 teaspoons stevia blend

Soak almonds in 4 cups of water overnight. Combine soaked almonds, water, and stevia in a blender. Puree on high speed for 2 minutes. Refrigerate unused portion. Keeps about 5 days.

Makes 5 cups.

Orange Jubilee

6 ounces frozen orange juice
concentrate
2¼ cups skim milk
½ teaspoon vanilla

8 each ice cubes
4 teaspoons stevia blend *or*
³/₈ tsp. stevioside
cinnamon and nutmeg, optional

Process orange juice concentrate, milk, vanilla, and stevia in a blender or food processor until smooth; add ice cubes and process until smooth and thick. Serve with sprinkles of nutmeg or cinnamon.

Makes 6 servings.

Strawberry Fizz

½ cup fresh strawberries
1 cup plain yogurt
2 teaspoons stevia blend *or*
¼ tsp. stevioside

¼ teaspoon vanilla
½ cup milk
½ cup sparkling water

In a blender, blend all ingredients, except the sparkling water, until well blended. Pour into glasses. Add sparkling water and gently stir into yogurt mixture. Serve immediately.

Makes 2 servings.

Peachy Yogurt Shake

1 each fresh peach, peeled and
   pitted
8 ounces plain nonfat yogurt
¹/₄ cup frozen orange juice
   concentrate

¹/₄ cup skim milk
2 teaspoons stevia blend *or*
   ¹/₄ tsp. stevioside
3 ice cubes

In a blender or food processor, combine yogurt, juice concentrate, milk, and stevia. Next, add peaches a few at a time. Puree till smooth, then add ice cubes one at a time through opening in lid, blending until thick. Pour into glasses and serve immediately.

Makes 3 servings.

Jungle Smoothie

2¹/₂ cups pineapple juice,
   unsweetened and chilled
1 cup strawberries
4 whole strawberries, for garnish
1 whole banana

1 whole mango
1 whole papaya
1 teaspoon stevia blend *or*
   ¹/₈ tsp. stevioside
1 cup skim milk

Peel, seed, and dice all of the fruit. Combine all ingredients in a blender or food processor. Puree until thick and very smooth. Serve in glasses garnished with a whole strawberry.

Makes 4 servings.

Beverages

Pineapple-Peach Smoothie

½ cup pineapple, chopped
1 cup plain yogurt
½ cup pineapple juice,
    unsweetened

1 cup skim milk
2 each peach halves
1 teaspoon stevia blend *or*
    ⅛ tsp. stevioside

Combine pineapple, pineapple juice, and peaches in blender or food processor; process until pureed. Add yogurt, milk, and stevia. Process until smooth. Pour into glasses, and serve immediately.

Makes 2 servings.

Stevia Fruit Smoothie

1 tablespoon oats
4 cups milk
½ medium papaya, peeled,
    seeded, and sliced
1 medium apple, peeled and sliced

1 each banana peeled and sliced
½ teaspoon vanilla
1 teaspoon stevia blend *or*
    ⅛ tsp. stevioside

In a blender, blend all of the fruit with a little milk until very smooth. Add remaining ingredients, and again blend until smooth. If desired, add a cup of crushed ice.

Makes 4 servings.

CHAPTER 6

Breads & Grains

BREADS & GRAINS

A Better Banana Nut Bread – 51

Banana Waffles – 61

Buckwheat Pancakes – 59

Buttermilk Pancakes – 59

Carrot Muffins – 52

Cheese Corn Bread – 49

Cinnamon Nut Waffles – 61

Cinnamon-Apple Puffed Oven Pancake – 60

French Toast – 57

Golden Corn Bread – 49

Healthy Biscuits – 47

Maple Breakfast Oatmeal – 58

Nutty Pancakes – 59

Oatmeal Wheat Muffins – 53

Pancakes – 59

Pumpkin Bread – 54

Soft and Sweet Dinner Rolls – 48

Southern Biscuits – 50

Tex-Mex Corn Bread – 49

Waffles – 61

Whole-Wheat Applesauce Muffins – 55

Zucchini or Apple Bread – 56

Healthy Biscuits

HIGH IN PROTEIN AND FLAVOR.

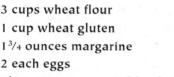

3 cups wheat flour
1 cup wheat gluten
1 3/4 ounces margarine
2 each eggs
2 1/4 teaspoons stevia blend *or*
   1/4 tsp. stevioside

1 package yeast
1/2 cup water, warm
1/2 teaspoon vanilla

Dissolve yeast and stevia in warm water. Beat margarine and eggs in a separate bowl. Stir in flour, and then add yeast mixture and vanilla. Let dough sit for 40 minutes. Roll out and cut into biscuits. Bake at 350°F for 30 minutes or until golden brown.

Makes about 24 biscuits.

Soft and Sweet
Dinner Rolls

1 cup milk

5 tablespoons butter

2 each eggs

3 teaspoons stevia blend *or*
  ³/₈ tsp. stevioside

1 teaspoon salt

4 cups all purpose flour

2¹/₂ teaspoons yeast

In a large mixing bowl, combine 2 cups of the flour and all the yeast. In a small saucepan, mix milk, stevia blend, butter, and salt. Stirring constantly, heat till warm and butter is almost melted. Add to flour mixture along with eggs. Beat with an electric mixer on low speed for 30 seconds, scraping bowl constantly. Beat on high speed for 3 minutes. Using a spoon, stir in as much of the remaining flour as you can until dough is only slightly sticky.

Turn dough out onto a lightly floured surface. Knead in enough remaining flour to make moderately stiff dough that is smooth and elastic. Shape dough into a ball. Place dough in a greased bowl; grease the dough completely. Cover and let rise in a warm place till double (about 1 hour).

Punch dough down. Turn out onto a lightly floured surface. Divide dough in half. Cover and let rest for 10 minutes. Shape the dough into desired rolls. Cover and let rise in a warm place till nearly double (about 30 minutes).

Bake in a 375°F oven for 12 to 15 minutes or till golden brown.

Makes 15–20 rolls.

Golden Corn Bread

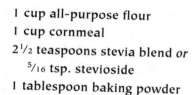

1 cup all-purpose flour
1 cup cornmeal
2 1/2 teaspoons stevia blend *or*
   5/16 tsp. stevioside
1 tablespoon baking powder

1 teaspoon salt
2 each eggs
1 cup milk
1/4 cup vegetable oil

In a mixing bowl, combine the flour, cornmeal, stevia blend, baking powder, and salt. Add the eggs, milk, and oil. Mix until batter is smooth. Pour into a greased 9 x 9 x 2-inch baking pan. Bake in a 425°F oven for 20 to 25 minutes or till golden brown.

Makes 8 servings.

Variations:

Cheese Corn Bread: Prepare as above, and stir in 1/2 cup shredded cheddar cheese.

Tex-Mex Corn Bread: Prepare as above, and stir in 3/4 cup picante sauce (see index).

Southern Biscuits

2 cups flour
1 tablespoon baking powder
1 teaspoon stevia blend *or*
   $^1/_8$ tsp. stevioside

$^1/_2$ teaspoon cream of tartar
1/4 teaspoon salt
$^1/_2$ cup shortening or butter
$^2/_3$ cup milk

In a bowl, stir together flour, baking powder, stevia, cream of tartar, and salt. Cut in shortening or butter till mixture resembles coarse crumbs. Add milk. Stir till just moist.

Knead dough on a lightly floured surface for 10 to 12 strokes. Roll dough to $^1/_2$-inch thickness. Cut with a biscuit cutter or inverted glass. Transfer biscuits to a greased baking sheet. Bake in a 450°F oven for 10 to 12 minutes or till golden. Serve Warm.

Makes 8–10 biscuits.

A Better
Banana Nut Bread

1 stick butter
2 each eggs
½ cup buttermilk
2 cups flour
½ teaspoon baking powder
¾ teaspoon baking soda

3 each ripe bananas
½ cup unsweetened applesauce,
1 teaspoon vanilla
1 teaspoon cinnamon, optional
2 teaspoons stevia blend *or*
   ¼ tsp. stevioside

In a large mixing bowl, mix all dry ingredients together. Set aside. In another bowl, mix all liquid ingredients together. Add the liquid mixture to the dry mixture and mix well. Pour into a well-greased loaf or cake pan. Bake at 350°F for 60–80 minutes or until done.

Makes 12 servings.

For a sweeter bread, add one extra teaspoon of stevia blend.

Carrot Muffins

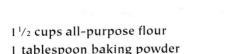

1 1/2 cups all-purpose flour
1 tablespoon baking powder
1/2 teaspoon baking soda
1/2 teaspoon ground cinnamon
1/2 teaspoon salt
2 each eggs
3 teaspoons stevia blend *or*
   3/8 tsp. stevioside

3/4 cup buttermilk
1/4 cup butter, melted
1 cup grated carrots
1/2 cup raisins, chopped
1/2 cup coarsely chopped walnuts

Mix flour, baking powder, cinnamon, salt, and stevia blend in a large bowl. Set aside. In a small mixing bowl, beat the eggs. Stir in carrots, raisins, and nuts. Gradually fold the flour mixture into the egg mixture till just moistened. Spoon batter into paper muffin cups or greased muffin tins. Bake 375°F for 20–25 minutes, or until muffin top springs back from a touch. Cool on a wire rack.

Makes about 12 muffins.

Breads & Grains

Oatmeal Wheat Muffins

1 cup whole wheat flour
1 1/2 cups rolled oats
1/2 teaspoon salt
3 teaspoons baking powder
1/2 teaspoon nutmeg
2 teaspoons cinnamon
1 1/2 teaspoons stevioside powder

2 each eggs
3/4 cup milk
1/4 cup oil
1 medium apple, cored and
    chopped
3/4 cup raisins, chopped

In a medium bowl, combine dry ingredients. Set aside. In a large mixing bowl, mix remaining ingredients. Gradually mix dry ingredients into moist ingredients. Spoon into greased muffin tins. Bake at 375°F for 15 to 20 minutes.

Makes about 12 muffins.

Pumpkin Bread

2 cups all-purpose flour
5 teaspoons stevia blend *or*
   5/8 tsp. stevioside
1 tablespoon molasses
1 tablespoon baking powder
1/2 teaspoon ground cinnamon
1/2 teaspoon salt
1/2 teaspoon ground nutmeg

1/4 teaspoon ground ginger
1 cup canned pumpkin
1/2 cup buttermilk
2 each eggs
1/3 cup margarine
1/2 cup chopped walnuts
1/2 cup raisins

In a large mixing bowl, combine 1 cup of the flour, the stevia blend, baking powder, cinnamon, salt, baking soda, nutmeg, and ginger. Add pumpkin, milk, eggs, shortening, and molasses. Beat with an electric mixer till well blended. Add remaining flour; beat well. Stir in nuts and raisins. Pour into a greased 9 x 5 x 3-inch loaf pan. Bake in a 350°F oven for 65 minutes or till toothpick inserted near the center comes out clean. Cool in pan for 10 minutes on a wire rack. Remove from the pan; cool thoroughly on a wire rack.

Makes 1 loaf.

Breads & Grains

Whole Wheat Applesauce Muffins

2 cups whole wheat flour
2 teaspoons baking powder
1/2 teaspoon baking soda
1 teaspoon ground cinnamon
1/2 teaspoon salt

2 each eggs, beaten
3 teaspoons stevia blend *or*
 3/8 tsp. stevioside
1 1/2 cups unsweetened applesauce
1/4 cup butter, melted

Mix flour, baking powder, cinnamon, stevia blend, and salt in a large bowl. Set aside. In a medium bowl, combine eggs, applesauce, and melted butter. Beat with an electric mixer on medium for 2 minutes or until well blended. Slowly add egg mixture to flour. Beat until combined. Spoon batter into paper muffin cups or a greased muffin tin. Bake 20–25 minutes at 375°F, or until brown and tops spring back from a touch.

Makes about 12 muffins.

Zucchini or Apple Bread

1 ½ cups all-purpose flour
1 teaspoon ground cinnamon
1 ½ teaspoons salt
¼ teaspoon baking powder
½ teaspoon ground nutmeg
5 teaspoons stevia blend *or*
   ⅝ tsp. stevioside

1 cup unpeeled zucchini or apple,
   finely shredded
¼ cup cooking oil
1 each egg
1 teaspoon lemon juice
½ cup chopped walnuts

In a mixing bowl, combine flour, stevia blend, cinnamon, baking soda, salt, baking powder, and nutmeg. In another mixing bowl, combine shredded zucchini or apple, cooking oil, egg, and lemon juice; mix well.

Add flour mixture to wet ingredients; stir just till combined. Stir in chopped walnuts. Pour batter into a greased 8 x 4 x 2-inch loaf pan. Bake in a 350°F oven for 55 to 60 minutes or until a toothpick inserted near the center comes out clean. Cool in pan for 10 minutes on a wire rack before turning out and cooling completely on wire rack.

Makes 1 loaf.

French Toast

For a custard type center use thick slices of French bread.
If you prefer a crisper French Toast use sliced white bread.

2 each eggs, beaten
$1/2$ cup milk
$1/2$ teaspoon vanilla
1 teaspoon stevia blend *or*
   $1/16$ teaspoon stevioside

$1/4$ teaspoon ground cinnamon
5 each 1-inch-thick slices French
   bread *or* 6 slices dry white
   bread
margarine, butter, or cooking oil

In a shallow bowl, beat together eggs, milk, vanilla, stevia, and cinnamon. Dip bread into egg mixture, coating both sides (if using French bread let it soak on both sides for 30 seconds).

In a skillet heat a small amount of margarine, butter, or cooking oil. Cook bread for 2 to 3 minutes on both sides or till golden brown. Add more oil as needed. Makes 5–6 pieces.

Serve with maple-flavored syrup or other topping if desired. (See *Tempting Toppings, Sweet Sauces, and Great Preserves.*)

Maple Breakfast Oatmeal

3 cups skim milk
1 1/2 cups quick-cooking oats
1/3 cup dried fruit bits or raisins
1 medium apple, peeled, cored,
   cubed
3 tablespoons unsalted sunflower
   seeds, toasted

1/3 teaspoon maple extract
5 teaspoons stevia blend *or*
   5/8 tsp. stevioside
2–3 dashes salt
ground cinnamon (optional)

Combine milk, oats, fruit bits, apple, sunflower seeds, stevia blend, salt, and maple extract in medium saucepan; heat to boiling over medium-high heat, stirring constantly. Reduce heat and simmer until thickened, 2 to 3 minutes. Spoon cereal into bowls; sprinkle with cinnamon.

Pancakes

1 ½ cups flour
1 teaspoon salt
2 ¼ teaspoons stevia blend *or*
   ¼ tsp. stevioside

2 teaspoons baking powder
2 each eggs, beaten
3 tablespoons melted butter
1 ¼ cups milk

Sift the flour with the salt, stevia, and baking powder into a mixing bowl. Make a well in the center of the flower mixture; add the eggs, melted butter, and milk. Stir until the batter is almost smooth and let stand at least 1 to 2 hours before cooking.

Lightly grease a frying pan with oil or butter. Pour batter onto hot skillet to make round cakes. Cook until bubbles appear on the surface and the underneath is brown. Turn pancake and brown other side. Serve hot.

Makes about 6 large pancakes.

Variations:

Buttermilk Pancakes: Prepare as above, substituting buttermilk for milk. If needed, add additional buttermilk to thin the batter.

Buckwheat Pancakes: Prepare as above, substituting ½ cup whole wheat flour and ½ cup buckwheat flour for the all-purpose flour.

Nutty Pancakes: Prepare as above, and fold ½ cup finely chopped nuts into the batter.

If desired, serve with Maple Flavored Syrup, Stevia Butter, Banana Sauce, Apricot Rum Sauce, Cherry Sauce, or Chocolate Sauce (see index).

Cinnamon Apple
Puffed Oven Pancake

Pancake:

4 each eggs
³/₄ cup skim milk
³/₄ cup all-purpose flour
2¹/₂ teaspoons stevia blend *or*
   ⁵/₁₆ tsp. stevioside
¹/₄ teaspoon salt
1 tablespoon margarine

Topping:

5 large cooking apples, sliced
2 tablespoons margarine
8 teaspoons stevia blend *or*
   1 tsp. stevioside
¹/₄ teaspoon ground cinnamon
¹/₈ teaspoon ground nutmeg
3 dashes ground allspice
1 tablespoon lemon juice
1 cup apple juice
4 teaspoons cornstarch
ground cinnamon

Pancake:

Mix eggs, milk, flour, 2¹/₂ teaspoons stevia blend, and salt in medium bowl (batter should be slightly lumpy). Heat 1 tablespoon margarine in 12-inch oven-proof skillet until bubbly; pour batter into skillet.

Bake pancake in preheated 425°F oven 20 minutes; reduce temperature to 350°F and bake until crisp and golden, 7 to 10 minutes (do not open oven door during baking). Transfer pancake to large serving plate.

Apple Topping:

Sauté apples in 2 tablespoons margarine in large skillet until apples begin to soften, 5 to 7 minutes. Mix in 8 teaspoons stevia blend, spices and lemon juice. Add ³/₄ cup cider and heat to boiling. Mix cornstarch and remaining ¹/₄ cup cider; add to boiling mixture, stirring until thickened (about 1 minute). Spoon apple mixture onto pancake. Sprinkle with cinnamon. Cut into wedges. Serves 6.

Waffles

1 3/4 cups all-purpose flour
1 tablespoon baking powder
1/4 teaspoon salt
2 1/2 teaspoons stevia blend *or*
   5/16 tsp. stevioside

2 each egg yolks
1 3/4 cups milk
1/2 cup cooking oil
2 each egg whites

In a mixing bowl, combine flour, baking powder, stevia, and salt. In another bowl, beat egg yolks. Add milk and oil; blend well. Combine egg yolk mixture with flour mixture all at once. Stir till just combined. Mixture should be slightly lumpy.

In a mixing bowl, beat egg whites till stiff peaks form. Gently fold beaten egg whites into flour and egg yolk mixture. Do not over mix.

Pour 1 cup of batter onto grids of a preheated, lightly greased waffle baker. Close lid quickly; do not open during baking. Bake according to manufacture's directions. When done, use a fork to lift waffle off grid. Repeat with remaining batter.

Makes 3 or 4 waffles.

Variations:

Fast Waffles: Do not separate eggs. Just beat whole eggs slightly then add milk and oil. Add to flour mixture all at once. Beat just till combined but still slightly lumpy.

Cinnamon-Nut Waffles: Prepare as above, adding 1/2 teaspoon ground cinnamon to flour mixture and sprinkling about 2 tablespoons chopped pecans over each waffle before closing lid to bake.

Banana Waffles: Prepare as above, reducing milk to 1 1/2 cups, and adding 1/4 teaspoon ground nutmeg and 2/3 cup mashed ripe banana to egg yolk mixture.

CHAPTER 7

Soups, Salads & Dressings

SOUPS, SALADS & DRESSINGS

 # Soups

Corn Chowder

1 10-oz. pkg. frozen, whole kernel corn	2 cups milk
1 cup potato, cubed & peeled	1 tablespoon butter
$^2/_3$ cup onion, chopped	$2^1/_2$ tablespoons flour
$^1/_2$ cup water	1 teaspoon stevia blend *or*
3 teaspoons instant, chicken bouillon granules	$^1/_8$ tsp. stevioside

In a large, heavy saucepan, combine frozen corn, potato, onion, water, and bouillon granules. Bring to a boil stirring occasionally; reduce heat. Cover and simmer till corn and potato are just tender, stirring occasionally. Stir in 1 $^1/_2$ cups of the milk, butter, and stevia. In a separate bowl, combine the remaining milk and flour. Stir milk-flour mixture into corn mixture. Cook, stirring constantly, till thickened and bubbly. Remove from heat, and serve hot.

Makes 6 servings.

Cream of Acorn Squash Soup

2 pounds acorn squash
1 1/2 cups chicken broth
1 tablespoon butter
1 tablespoon flour
1/4 teaspoon ground ginger

1 teaspoon stevia blend *or*
  1/16 teaspoon stevioside
1 cup milk
salt and pepper to taste

Wash, halve, and remove seeds from squash. Place halves, cut-side-down, in a baking dish. Bake at 350°F for 45 minutes or till tender. Cool slightly. Remove skin and cube. Combine the cooked squash and 3/4 cup of the broth in a blender or food processor. Puree till smooth. Set aside. In a saucepan, melt margarine. Stir in flour, ginger, and stevia. Stir in milk. Stirring constantly, cook until thick and bubbly. Stir in squash puree and remaining broth. Continue stirring, and cook till heated through. Salt and pepper to taste.

Makes 4 servings.

Soups, Salads & Dressings

Tomato Soup With Herbs

3/4 cup onion, sliced

2 tablespoons butter

2 cups tomatoes, chopped &
   peeled or

1 14 1/2-ounce can whole, peeled
   tomatoes, cup up

1 1/2 cups vegetable broth

1 8-ounce can tomato sauce

1 tablespoon fresh, snipped basil

2 teaspoons fresh, snipped thyme

1 teaspoon stevia blend or
   1/8 tsp. stevioside

In a large, heavy saucepan, sauté onion in butter until tender. Add fresh tomatoes or undrained canned tomatoes, broth, tomato sauce, basil, thyme, and stevia. Stirring occasionally bring to boiling; reduce heat. Cover and simmer for 30 minutes stirring occasionally. Cool slightly. Puree soup in batches in a blender or food processor till smooth. Return mixture to saucepan; heat through.

Makes 4 servings.

 *Salads*

Carrot-Raisin Salad

3 medium carrots, shredded
1 small apple, peeled, seeded, &
    chopped
$^1/_3$ cup raisins

1 teaspoon lemon juice
$^1/_3$ cup mayonnaise
1 $^1/_2$ teaspoons stevia blend *or*
    $^3/_{16}$ tsp. stevioside

In a bowl, combine lemon juice, stevia, and mayonnaise; mix well. Add shredded carrots, chopped apple, and raisins. Mix well. Chill for at least 2 hours.

Makes 6 servings.

Corn Salad

1 16-oz can corn, drained
1/2 cup sweet onion, finely
   chopped
2 each tomatoes, chopped
2 each green bell peppers,
   chopped

1/4 cup celery, chopped
1 1/2 teaspoons stevia blend *or*
   3/16 tsp. stevioside
1 tablespoon apple cider vinegar
1/4 cup mayonnaise

In a small bowl, whisk vinegar, mayonnaise, and stevia till well blended. In a medium bowl, combine corn, onion, tomatoes, bell peppers, and celery. Stir in vinegar mixture. Chill for several hours before serving.

Makes 4 servings.

Cucumber Salad

2 large cucumbers, sliced
$1/3$ cup onion, finely chopped
1 teaspoon stevia blend or
$1/8$ tsp. stevioside
$1/4$ cup apple cider vinegar
$1/2$ teaspoon dry basil, crushed

$1/2$ teaspoon celery seed
$1/2$ teaspoon dry dill weed
$1/4$ cup celery, finely chopped
$1/4$ cup olive oil
salt and pepper, to taste

In a small bowl, combine stevia, vinegar, basil, celery seed, and dill. Mix well. In a large bowl, combine cucumbers, onion, and celery. Add vinegar mixture and oil. Toss to coat. Chill at least 1 hour before serving.

Makes 6 servings.

Summer Coleslaw

¼ cup red bell pepper, chopped
¼ cup yellow bell pepper, chopped
½ cup carrot, chopped
⅓ cup red onion, chopped
8 ounces cheddar cheese, shredded
2½ cups green cabbage, thinly sliced

2½ cups red cabbage, thinly sliced
1 tablespoon red wine vinegar
6 teaspoons stevia blend *or* ¾ tsp. stevioside
½ cup mayonnaise
¼ teaspoon celery seed
salt and pepper, to taste

Mix vegetables and cheese in bowl. Mix stevia, vinegar, mayonnaise, and celery seed in a separate bowl. Stir into vegetables. Season with salt and pepper. Refrigerate till chilled.

Makes 8 servings.

German-Style Potato Salad

4 medium potatoes, peeled,
  boiled, and cubed
4 slices bacon
1/2 cup onion, chopped
1 tablespoon vegetable oil
1 tablespoon flour
1 1/2 teaspoons stevia blend *or*
  3/16 tsp. stevioside

1 teaspoon salt
1/2 teaspoon celery seed
1/8 teaspoon pepper
1/2 cup water
1/4 cup apple cider vinegar
1 each hard-boiled egg, sliced

Cook potatoes in boiling water till tender; drain well. Cool; peel and slice potatoes. Set aside.

Dressing:

Cook 4 slices bacon till crisp. Drain and crumble; set aside. Cook onions in vegetable oil till tender. Stir in flour, stevia, salt, celery seed, and pepper. Stir in vinegar and water. Stirring constantly, cook until thick and bubbly. Add potatoes and bacon. Still stirring constantly, cook for 5 minutes more. Spoon into a serving bowl, and garnish with hard-boiled egg.

Makes 4 servings.

Lemon and Herb Mushroom Salad

½ pound fresh whole mushrooms
3 tablespoons lemon juice
2 tablespoons salad oil
1 tablespoon crushed garlic
1 teaspoon stevia blend *or*
   ⅛ tsp. stevioside

1/4 teaspoon salt
¼ teaspoon pepper
⅛ teaspoon oregano
⅛ teaspoon thyme
½ small red onion, thinly sliced
¼ cup celery, finely chopped

In a medium saucepan, blanch mushrooms in boiling water for 1 minute. Drain and rinse with cold water; drain again. In a bowl, combine mushrooms and onions. Set aside.

Marinade:

In a small saucepan, combine lemon juice, salad oil, stevia, garlic, and spices. Cook till boiling stirring occasionally. Reduce heat and simmer, uncovered, 5 minutes stirring occasionally. Pour hot marinade over mushrooms and onions; toss till coated. Cover; chill at least 8 hours, stirring occasionally.

Makes 6 servings.

Shrimp Salad

1 cup shrimp, cooked
4 ounces cream cheese
2 large tomatoes, finely diced
2 tablespoons mayonnaise

$^1/_2$ teaspoon garlic powder
1 $^1/_2$ teaspoons stevia blend *or*
   $^3/_{16}$ tsp. stevioside
$^1/_4$ cup onion, minced

In a large bowl, mix all ingredients but the tomatoes. Gently stir in tomatoes. Refrigerate, and serve chilled. Can be served on a bed of lettuce, as an appetizer on crackers, or mixed with cooked pasta as a salad.

No Chicken Salad

3 cups seitan, cooked (or textured vegetable protein)
1 cup celery, diced
1 8-ounce can water chestnuts, diced
3 each green onions, minced
1 1/4 cups green grapes, cut in half
2 tablespoons fresh tarragon, minced

4 tablespoons fresh parsley, minced
2 teaspoons Dijon mustard
1 each lemon, juice of and zest
1 teaspoon stevia blend
1/8 tsp. stevioside
14 ounces salad dressing or mayonnaise
salt and pepper to taste

In a small bowl, dissolve stevia into the lemon juice. Set aside. In a large bowl, combine all other ingredients. Add lemon-stevia mixture; mix well. Refrigerate at least 2 hours. Use over greens, in a sandwich, or with crackers.

Makes about 6 cups or about 4 servings.

Greek Pasta Shrimp Salad

8 ounces rotelle pasta
12 ounces small shrimp, cooked
2 tablespoons red onion, minced
1 each celery stalk, finely chopped
1/3 cup olives, chopped
1/4 teaspoon red pepper
10 each cherry tomatoes
3/4 cup asiago cheese, finely grated

2 teaspoons stevia blend *or*
 1/4 tsp. stevioside
1/4 cup lemon juice
1/4 cup olive oil
2 cloves garlic, minced
1/4 teaspoon dried mustard
salt & pepper to taste

Cook pasta according to package instructions. Toss cooked pasta in a large bowl with shrimp, onion, olives, and celery. In a smaller bowl, combine oil, juice, stevia, garlic, pepper, mustard, and salt. Mix well or use a blender. Pour dressing over pasta and mix well. Garnish with tomatoes and asiago cheese.

Makes 4 servings.

Soups, Salads & Dressings

Pasta Salad

4 cups ham, cubed
1 pound rotini pasta, cooked
6 ounces olives, pitted
4 medium carrots, cooked, sliced
1 medium green bell pepper,
  sliced
1 medium red bell pepper, sliced

1 medium yellow bell pepper, sliced
1 tablespoon garlic, minced
1 tablespoon Italian seasoning
1 cup Italian Dressing (see index)
2 teaspoons stevia blend *or*
  $^1/_4$ tsp. stevioside
salt and pepper, to taste

Cook pasta according to instructions. Drain. Place cooked pasta in a large bowl. Add cubed ham, sliced vegetables, olives, spices, and Italian dressing; toss till coated and mixed well. Chill at least 4 hours for seasonings to blend.

Makes 6 servings.

Dijon Tofu Wilted Salad

½ pound tofu, frozen then defrosted
½ teaspoon salt
¼ teaspoon ground black pepper

1 head romaine lettuce, washed and torn into small pieces
1 cup Dijon Vinaigrette (see index)
olive oil for browning

Allow tofu to thaw; gently squeeze out excess water. (This process gives tofu a firm, slightly chewy texture.) Cut tofu into 1-inch cubes. In a skillet, lightly sauté tofu in a small amount of oil until light brown. Sprinkle with salt and pepper.

Make a bed of lettuce on a large plate. Spoon sautéed tofu on top of lettuce. Drizzle Dijon dressing over the tofu and serve.

Makes 4 servings.

Orange-Spinach Toss

3 cups fresh spinach, washed & torn
2 each oranges, peeled and
   sectioned
1 cup sliced, fresh mushrooms
2 tablespoons salad oil
1 teaspoon lemon juice

1 tablespoon orange juice
1 teaspoon stevia blend *or*
   $^1/_8$ tsp. stevioside
$^1/_4$ teaspoon poppy seeds
$^1/_8$ teaspoon garlic powder
$^1/_4$ cup toasted, slivered almonds

Place spinach in a large salad bowl. Add oranges and mushrooms. Toss lightly to mix.

Dressing:

In a screw-top jar, combine salad oil, lemon juice, stevia, poppy seeds, and garlic powder. Cover and shake well. Pour the dressing over the salad. Toss lightly to coat. Sprinkle with toasted almonds. Makes 4 servings.

Melon Salad

4 each navel oranges, peeled,
   seeded, & sliced
1 each cantaloupe, peeled, seeded,
   & sliced
1 each honeydew melon, peeled,
   seeded, & sliced

1 cup Cream Cheese Dressing (see
   index)
1 tablespoon lemon juice
stevia blend to taste

Combine fruit in a large bowl. Sprinkle with lemon juice. Keep refrigerated until ready to serve. Sprinkle with stevia blend if desired. Top with Cream Cheese Dressing (see index).

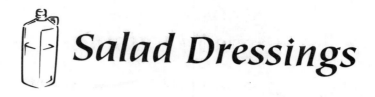 **Salad Dressings**

Ginger Vinaigrette

¹/₂ cup vegetable oil
¹/₃ cup white wine vinegar
³/₄ teaspoon stevia blend *or*
   ³/₃₂ tsp. stevioside

1 teaspoon fresh grated ginger root
¹/₂ teaspoon paprika
¹/₈ teaspoon pepper

Combine all ingredients in a screw-top jar. Cover and shake well. Keeps for up to 2 weeks. Shake before serving.

Makes about 1 cup.

Dijon Vinaigrette

¹/₂ cup olive oil
¹/₂ teaspoon paprika
1 teaspoon stevia blend *or*
   ¹/₈ tsp. stevioside

¹/₄ cup Dijon-style mustard
¹/₄ cup balsamic vinegar
1 clove garlic, minced
¹/₄ teaspoon pepper

In a screw-top jar, combine all ingredients. Cover, shake well. Keeps in the refrigerator for up to 1 week. Shake before serving.

Makes 1 cup.

Italian Dressing

2 tablespoons parmesan cheese, grated
1/2 teaspoon stevia blend *or* 1/16 tsp. stevioside
1/8 teaspoon salt
1/8 teaspoon pepper
1 tablespoon onion, minced

3 tablespoons parsley, minced
1 tablespoon basil, fresh, minced
1 tablespoon marjoram, minced
1/2 teaspoon celery seeds
1 clove garlic, minced
1/3 cup white wine vinegar
3/4 cup olive oil

In a screw-top jar, combine all ingredients. Cover, shake well. Keeps in the refrigerator up to 1 week. Shake before serving.

Makes 1 cup.

Poppy Seed Dressing

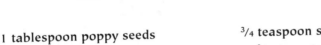

1 tablespoon poppy seeds
1/4 teaspoon dry mustard
2 tablespoons water
1/4 teaspoon onion powder

3/4 teaspoon stevia blend *or* 3/32 tsp. stevioside
2 tablespoons apple cider vinegar
1/2 cup sour cream

In a small saucepan, combine poppy seeds, mustard, water, onion powder, and stevia. Heat just till boiling stirring occasionally. Remove from heat. Allow to cool slightly. Add vinegar and yogurt. Pour into an airtight container; keep refrigerated until needed, up to 5 days.

Makes about 1/2 cup.

Soups, Salads & Dressings

Creamy Salad Dressing

**THIS RICH AND CREAMY DRESSING IS PERFECT
FOR GREENS OR FRUIT.**

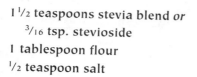

1 1/2 teaspoons stevia blend *or*
   3/16 tsp. stevioside
1 tablespoon flour
1/2 teaspoon salt

1/2 teaspoon dry mustard
3/4 cup milk
2 each egg yolks, slightly beaten
1/4 cup white wine vinegar

Combine stevia, flour, salt, and mustard in a saucepan. Add milk and egg yolks. Stirring constantly, cook until thick and bubbly. Continue cooking and stirring 2 more minutes. Add vinegar; stir till smooth. Pour into an airtight container; keep refrigerated until needed, up to 2 weeks.

Makes about 1 cup.

Creamy Garlic Dressing

¹/₄ cup skim milk
³/₄ cup skim milk, hot
1 cup sour cream
1 teaspoon gelatin powder
2 teaspoons stevia blend *or*
   ¹/₄ tsp. stevioside

¹/₂ teaspoon garlic powder
¹/₄ cup parsley
¹/₄ teaspoon salt
¹/₈ teaspoon pepper

In a blender, sprinkle unflavored gelatin over cold milk; let stand 2 minutes. Add hot milk and process at low speed until gelatin is completely dissolved. Add remaining ingredients and process at high speed until blended. Pour into an airtight container; keep refrigerated until needed, up to 5 days. Shake well before using.

Makes 2 cups.

Cinnamon Fruit Dressing

PERFECT FOR DIPPING APPLES.

8 ounces sour cream
¹/₄ cup apricot sugar-free
   preserves (spreadable fruit)

1 ¹/₂ teaspoons stevia blend *or*
   ³/₁₆ tsp. stevioside
¹/₄ teaspoon ground cinnamon

In a bowl, combine all ingredients. Mix well. Chill for several hours before serving. Serve with your favorite fruit.

Makes 1¹/₄ cups.

Cream Cheese Fruit Dressing

MAKES A GREAT DIP.

4 ounces cream cheese, room
  temperature
1/2 cup sour cream
2 tablespoons mayonnaise
1 teaspoon cinnamon

1 teaspoon allspice
2 teaspoons stevia blend *or*
  1/4 tsp. stevioside
1 teaspoon vanilla

Combine all ingredients in a large mixing bowl. With an electric mixer, beat till smooth and creamy. Chill at least 1 hour before serving. Serve with your favorite fruit. Keeps up to 2 weeks in refrigerator. *Makes about 1 cup.*

Sour Cream Fruit Dressing

MAKES A GREAT DIP.

8 ounces sour cream
1/4 cup apricot spreadable fruit or
  Sugar-Free Jam (see index)

1 teaspoon stevia blend *or*
  1/8 tsp. stevioside
1/8 teaspoon ground cinnamon

In a small bowl, blend all ingredients well. Chill for several hours or overnight. Serve with your favorite fruit.

CHAPTER 8

Vegetables

VEGETABLES

Gingered Vegetables

1 pound fresh broccoli florets
1 pound fresh mini peeled carrots
4 each yellow crook neck squash,
   cut in ½-inch diagonal slices

Sauce:

1/2 cup butter
1 teaspoon stevia blend

⅛ tsp. stevioside
1 teaspoon ground ginger
½ teaspoon chopped garlic
2 teaspoons frozen orange juice
   concentrate
1 tablespoon soy sauce
salt and pepper to taste

In a large saucepan, boil 3 cups of water. Add the carrots; boil, covered, for 3 minutes. Then add the broccoli; boil, covered, for 3 minutes. Add the squash last; boil, covered, 3 minutes. Drain. Transfer to a serving bowl.

Sauce:

In a small saucepan, melt butter. Stir in all remaining ingredients. Over medium heat, cook for 3 minutes stirring constantly. Pour sauce over vegetables. Toss lightly.

Makes 8 servings.

Sweet-and-Sour Carrots

1 16-oz. bag carrots
4 each green onions, cut into
  ¹/₂-inch pieces
¹/₂ cup unsweetened pineapple juice
3 teaspoons stevia blend *or*
  ³/₈ tsp. stevioside

2 tablespoons butter
1 tablespoon apple cider vinegar
1 ¹/₂ teaspoons cornstarch
1 teaspoon soy sauce

Cut carrots into thin slices. Steam about 5–10 minutes until tender but crispy. Meanwhile, in a saucepan, combine onions, juice, stevia, butter, vinegar, cornstarch, and soy sauce. Mix well. Stirring constantly, cook till bubbly. Add carrots. Continue cooking and stirring till heated, but be careful not to overcook.

Makes 4 servings.

Maple Glazed Carrots

³/₄ pound small carrots, peeled
1 tablespoon butter
¹/₂ teaspoon maple flavoring

1 teaspoon stevia blend *or*
  ¹/₈ tsp. stevioside

Cut carrots in half both lengthwise and crosswise. In a saucepan, boil fresh carrots, covered, for 7–10 minutes or till crisp-tender. Drain and remove carrots. In the same pan, melt butter. Add flavoring and stevia. Mix well. Add cooked carrots. Heat through.

Makes 4 servings.

Vegetables

Harvest Time Beets

4 medium beets
2 teaspoons stevia blend *or*
   $1/4$ tsp. stevioside

2 tablespoons vinegar
2 teaspoons cornstarch
1 tablespoon butter

Cook fresh, well-scrubbed, whole beets in boiling water for 40 to 50 minutes or till tender. Drain, reserving $1/3$ cup liquid. Skin and dice beets. In a saucepan, combine reserved liquid, stevia, vinegar, and cornstarch. Stirring constantly, cook until thick and bubbly. Continue cooking and stirring 2 more minutes. Stir in beets and margarine.

Makes 4 servings.

German Red Cabbage

2 cups red cabbage, shredded
1 small onion, chopped
1 tablespoon stevia blend *or*
   $1/8$ tsp. stevioside
2 tablespoons apple cider vinegar
$1/2$ cup apple juice

2 tablespoons butter
6 slices bacon, cooked and
   crumbled
2 each red apples, cored and
   coarsely chopped
salt and pepper to taste

In a Dutch oven, melt butter; add stevia, vinegar, and juice; mix well. Add cooked bacon, onion, and shredded cabbage. Cook, covered, over medium-low heat for 20–30 minutes, or till tender.

Makes 4 servings.

Three-Bean Bake

1 cup chopped onion
6 slices bacon, cut up
1 clove garlic, minced
2 16-oz. cans navy beans, drained
1 16-oz. can red kidney beans, drained
1 16-oz. can garbanzo beans, drained
1 cup catsup (for sugar-free catsup, see index)

9 teaspoons stevia blend *or* 1 ⅛ tsp. stevioside
¼ cup water
1 teaspoon maple flavoring
1 tablespoon prepared yellow mustard
1 tablespoon Worcestershire sauce

Cook chopped onion, bacon, and garlic in a skillet till bacon is done. In a heavy casserole dish, combine cooked onion, bacon, and garlic mixture and all other ingredients. Bake in a 350°F oven about 60 minutes; stirring occasionally.

Makes 8 servings.

Cinnamon Glazed Acorn Squash

1 medium acorn squash
3 teaspoons stevia blend *or*
  ³/₈ tsp. stevioside

1 tablespoon butter
1 teaspoon lemon juice
¹/₄ teaspoon cinnamon

Cut squash into 8 wedges; remove seeds. Arrange in a single layer on baking dish. Bake, covered, in a 350°F oven for 40 minutes. While squash is cooking, in a saucepan, combine stevia, margarine, lemon juice, and cinnamon. Stirring constantly, cook until bubbly. Spoon over baked squash. Bake squash, uncovered, about 10 minutes longer. Baste often.

Makes 4 servings.

Maple Glazed Sweet Potatoes

3 medium sweet potatoes
3 teaspoons stevia blend *or*
   ³/₈ tsp. stevioside

¹/₂ teaspoon maple flavor 2
   tablespoons butter

Boil fresh sweet potatoes for 25 to 35 minutes or until tender. Drain; cool slightly. Peel and cut into ¹/₂-inch thick slices. Transfer to serving bowl. In a small saucepan melt butter. Add stevia and maple flavor. Stir till stevia dissolves. Drizzle warm butter mixture over cooked sweet potatoes. Toss lightly.

Makes 4 servings.

Sweet Potato Casserole

3 large sweet potatoes, peeled,
   cooked and mashed
3 teaspoons stevia blend *or*
   ³/₈ teaspoon stevioside
¹/₂ cup melted butter
2 each eggs, slightly beaten
1 teaspoon vanilla
¹/₃ cup milk

Topping:

¹/₂ cup melted butter
¹/₂ cup flour
3 teaspoons stevia blend *or*
   ³/₈ tsp. stevioside
1 cup chopped pecans

In a small bowl, combine 3 tsp. stevia, ¹/₂ cup melted butter, eggs, vanilla and milk. Mix well. In a large casserole dish, combine sweet potatoes with milk mixture. Mix well.

For topping:

In a small bowl, mix the flour, 3 tsp. stevia, and pecans. Add ¹/₂ cup melted butter to the flour mixture. Sprinkle topping over sweet potato casserole. Bake at 350°F for 25 minutes.

Makes 6 side-dish servings.

CHAPTER 9

Main Dishes

MAIN DISHES

Barbecue-Style Beef

**THE GREAT TASTE OF AN OUTDOOR BARBECUE
WITH THE EASE OF OVEN ROASTING**

1 2 to 3-pound beef, chuck pot
   roast or brisket
2 tablespoons margarine or butter
2 medium onions, chopped
2 cloves garlic, minced

1 cup Mustard Barbecue Sauce
   (see index)
1 teaspoon chili powder
oil for browning

Rub salt and pepper on meat. In a Dutch oven, brown meat on all
sides in oil. Remove meat; replace with onions and garlic, and cook till
tender but not brown. Stir in barbecue sauce, chili powder, and ½ cup
water. Add meat. Bring to boiling, then reduce heat; cover and simmer
for 1 to 2 hours or till meat is tender. Remove meat. Cut into slices
against the grain of the meat.

Serves 8.

Beef Tenderloins & Greens

1 pound beef tenderloin	¹/₄ teaspoon ground black pepper
1 tablespoon olive oil	1 head romaine lettuce
¹/₂ teaspoon salt	1 cup Dijon Vinaigrette (see index)

Brush beef with olive oil. Rub in salt and pepper; place on a hot grill. Grill both sides till meat is cooked to your preference. Remove from grill and cut into 1" cubes. Wash romaine lettuce and chop into small squares. Arrange lettuce on individual plates. Place beef over lettuce. Spoon Dijon dressing over beef and lettuce.

Serves 4.

Pineapple Chicken

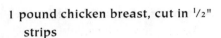

1 pound chicken breast, cut in ¹/₂"
  strips
1 tablespoon soy sauce
¹/₂ teaspoon cornstarch
2 each bell peppers, cut in fine strips
1 clove garlic, minced
1 8-ounce can pineapple chunks
  in juice

1 tablespoon tomato paste
2 teaspoons stevia blend *or*
  ¹/₄ tsp. stevioside
1 tablespoon soy sauce
1 teaspoon Worcestershire sauce
vegetable oil for cooking

Slice chicken into strips. Place in bowl, and add 1 tablespoon soy sauce and cornstarch. Toss and allow to marinate in refrigerator for at least 1 hour.

For sauce: In a bowl, mix tomato paste, stevia, 1 tablespoon soy sauce, pineapple, and Worcestershire sauce. Set aside.

Sweet & Sour Chicken

1 pound chicken, cut in 1" cubes
1 tablespoon soy sauce
1 each egg white
³/₄ cup cornstarch
¹/₂ teaspoon ginger
¹/₂ each red bell pepper, cut in thin strips
¹/₂ each green bell pepper, cut in thin strips
1 8-ounce can pineapple chunks, drained, reserve juice
oil for frying

Sweet and Sour Sauce

1 cup water
4 tablespoons stevia blend *or* 1 ¹/₂ tsp. stevioside
¹/₄ cup white vinegar
¹/₄ cup tomato sauce
2 tablespoons cornstarch
¹/₂ cup pineapple juice
4 cups cooked rice

Chicken:

In a bowl, combine 1 tablespoon soy sauce, egg white, and ³/₄ cup cornstarch. Coat cubed chicken in cornstarch mixture. Heat oil in wok or deep frying pan. Drop in chicken a few pieces at a time. Deep-fry until crispy and golden brown on all sides. Remove chicken with a slotted spoon, and place on absorbent material. Retain about 2 tablespoons of oil in wok or frying pan. Stir-fry red and green peppers for 1 minute.

Sauce:

In a medium saucepan, combine water, stevia, pineapple juice, vinegar, and tomato juice. Bring to boil stirring constantly. Dissolve 2 tablespoons cornstarch in 1 cup cold water. Stir cornstarch-water into hot pineapple mixture. Cook over medium heat stirring constantly till thick. Add peppers and pineapple chunks to sauce. Pour sauce over chicken and serve with rice.

Makes 4 servings.

Variations:

Substitute cubed pork, shrimp, or vegetables for chicken.

In a large skillet, heat 2 tablespoons water over medium-high heat. Add peppers and garlic; sauté for 3–4 minutes. Remove from skillet; set aside. Clean skillet. Heat oil in clean skillet. Add chicken and stir-fry 3–4 minutes or till golden on all sides. Add sauce to pan; bring to a low boil stirring constantly. Add cooked peppers. Serve hot over cooked rice.

Makes 4 servings.

Italian Chicken

4 chicken breasts, boned and
  skinned
1 1/2 tablespoon olive oil
3 cloves garlic, halved
4 bay leaves
1 teaspoon ground ginger
2 teaspoons stevia blend *or*
  1/8 teaspoon stevioside

1/2 cup balsamic vinegar
1/3 cup dry white wine
1/2 lemon
1 orange
salt and pepper to taste
1 (24 x 17-inch) sheet parchment
  paper
1 tablespoon pine nuts

Flour chicken breasts and set aside. In a 12-inch non-stick pan, heat olive oil over medium-high heat and sauté chicken breasts with garlic, bay leaves and ginger until chicken is golden. Be careful not to burn the garlic. Remove breasts from pan and set aside. In pan, add stevia, vinegar and wine to pan; reduce mixture by half. Add juices, salt and pepper, and reduce again by two-thirds. Discard bay leaf.

Place parchment paper on a shallow roasting pan. Place chicken breasts on one-half of paper. Sprinkle pine nuts over chicken and spoon sauce over breasts. Fold parchment paper over the top of the chicken. Crimp the edges together until you have an airtight seal. Place in a preheated oven at 375° F for 25 minutes. Remove promptly and serve hot.

Curry Chicken

1/3 cup butter or margarine
1 tablespoon curry powder
1 teaspoon salt
2 teaspoons stevia blend *or*
   1/4 tsp. stevioside
2 cups milk
1 teaspoon lemon juice

1/2 cup onion, finely chopped
1/3 cup wheat flour
1/4 teaspoon ginger
2 cups chicken broth
4 cups cooked rice
1 pound chicken breasts, boned &
   skinned
chopped chives, for garnish

Sauce:

Melt butter in a saucepan over low heat. Be careful not to burn the butter. Sauté onion until clear; add curry powder and stir until well mixed. Stir in flour, salt, ginger, and stevia. Cook, stirring constantly, over medium-low heat for 3 minutes. Remove from heat; gradually at first, stir in milk and broth. Return to heat and bring to a low boil, stirring constantly until thick. Remove from heat.

Chicken:

Melt 2 teaspoons butter in a skillet. Lightly flour chicken pieces and sauté in skillet until brown on both sides and cooked through.

Make a bed of rice on each plate; place chicken on top of rice. Spoon sauce over chicken. If desired, sprinkle chopped chives over prepared dish.

Serves 4.

Variations:

Substitute shrimp, beef, or your favorite vegetables for chicken.

Sweet and Spicy Buffalo Chicken

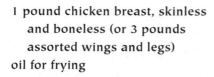

1 pound chicken breast, skinless and boneless (or 3 pounds assorted wings and legs)
oil for frying

Coating for chicken:

1 cup flour
1 teaspoon salt
1 teaspoon garlic powder
1 teaspoon onion powder
1/2 teaspoon ground black pepper
1 teaspoon ground cayenne pepper

Sauce:

1/4 cup ghee* clarified cutter
1 tablespoon Tabasco sauce or your favorite hot sauce
1/8 cup vinegar
1 tablespoon powdered milk
1/4 cup tomato sauce
1/4 tablespoon cornstarch
2 teaspoons stevia blend or 1/4 tsp. stevioside
1/4 teaspoon salt
1/2 teaspoon garlic powder
1/2 teaspoon onion powder
1/4 teaspoon cilantro

Mix coating ingredients in a bowl. Add sliced chicken to flour mix and coat very well. Place coated chicken on a plate and refrigerate for 45 minutes. Re-coat chicken in flour mix and refrigerate another 45 minutes.

Sauce:

Melt ghee in a saucepan. Add garlic, onion, and cilantro; sauté till onions are tender. Set aside. In another saucepan, combine Tabasco, salt, tomato sauce, powdered milk, stevia, and vinegar and let simmer 5 minutes. Add this mixture to the ghee mixture and bring to a boil stirring constantly until thick. Remove from heat and allow to cool. In a frying pan, heat oil, and fry chicken until golden brown. Remove chicken and place in a round-bottom bowl. Add sauce and toss chicken until well coated. Serve hot.

If you like it spicy, add more Tabasco, ground jalapenos, or try my favorite, ground Habanero peppers; just add your choice to the ghee while its melting.

Variation:

Buffalo Vegetables: Slice an onion, a zucchini, a yellow squash, a few large jalapenos and any other vegetables that you like. Coat with flour, and fry until crispy and brown. Toss in sauce till well-coated.

---

*Ghee is clarified butter that does not burn like normal butter, available at your local health food store or international market. You may substitute butter but watch for burning.

Crab Cakes

1 1/2 pounds crab meat
6 tablespoons butter
1 each small onion, finely
  chopped
1 1/2 cups dry bread crumbs
3 each eggs, slightly beaten
1/4 cup parsley
1 teaspoon dry mustard
1 teaspoon paprika

1/2 teaspoon salt
1/4 teaspoon ground black pepper
1/4 cup heavy cream
2 teaspoons stevia blend *or*
  1/4 tsp. stevioside
1 each apple, peeled, cored, and
  chopped
flour to coat cakes
oil for frying

In a small bowl, dissolve stevia into cream. Set aside. Melt butter in a large saucepan. Sauté onions in butter until clear. Add crab meat, and cook for 5 minutes. In a large bowl, combine crab mix with eggs, parsley, dry mustard, paprika, salt, pepper, and apple. Add cream and stevia mixture to crab mixture. Slowly stir in bread crumbs until moist, firm texture is reached. Shape into small cakes, and coat lightly with flour. Heat a small amount of oil in a frying pan, and fry cake until golden brown. Turn and fry other side till golden.

Makes 12 cakes.

Serve hot with cocktail sauce (see index).

Balsamic Medallions

1 pound seitan*	1/4 cup balsamic vinegar
1 1/2 tablespoons olive oil	1/3 cup dry white wine
3 cloves garlic	1/2 each lemon
4 each bay leaves	1 each orange
1 teaspoon ground ginger	1 tablespoon pine nuts
2 teaspoons stevia blend *or*	salt and pepper to taste
1/4 tsp. stevioside	parchment paper

Prepare seitan or textured vegetable protein according to manufacture's directions. Divide into 4 medium-size patties. Sauté the patties in olive oil with garlic, bay leaves, and ginger over medium-high heat until lightly brown and firm. Be careful not to burn the garlic. Remove patties from the pan and set aside. Reduce heat, and add stevia, vinegar, and wine to pan. Cook until reduced by half. Add the juice from 1/2 lemon and 1 orange; salt and pepper to taste. Allow sauce to simmer for about 15 minutes stirring occasionally. Discard garlic and bay leaves.

Place parchment paper on a shallow roasting pan. Place patties on one-half of paper. Add pine nuts, and spoon sauce over patties. Fold parchment paper over the top of the patties. Crimp edges together until you have a tight seal. Place in a 400°F oven for 12 minutes. Remove promptly, and serve.

Makes 4 servings.

---

*seitan is avalible at health food stores.

Chili

VEGETARIAN

2 (16-ounce) cans kidney beans, drained
1 cup onion, chopped
2 each small red or green peppers, cubed
2 stalks celery, chopped
1 teaspoon cumin
1 tablespoon lime juice
1 cup zucchini, cubed

3 tablespoons olive oil
2 cloves garlic, chopped
1 each carrot, chopped
2 tablespoons chili powder
1 can whole tomatoes
8 ounces shredded cheddar cheese
2 teaspoons stevia blend *or*
    1/4 tsp. stevioside

Puree 1 can of beans in a food processor. In a Dutch oven, heat oil and sauté onion and garlic. Add green peppers, carrot, and celery. Stir in chili powder and cumin. Cook, stirring occasionally for 10 minutes. Add tomatoes, pureed beans, whole beans, stevia, and zucchini. Allow to simmer for 20 minutes, stirring often. Spoon into bowls, and sprinkle with cheese.

Main Dishes

Seitan Cakes

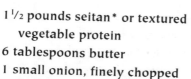

1 ½ pounds seitan* or textured
    vegetable protein
6 tablespoons butter
1 small onion, finely chopped
1 ½ cups bread crumbs
3 each eggs, slightly beaten
¼ cup parsley, finely chopped
1 teaspoon dry mustard

1 teaspoon paprika
½ teaspoon salt and pepper
¼ cup heavy cream
2 teaspoons stevia blend *or*
    ¼ teaspoon stevioside
1 each apple, seeded and chopped
flour to coat cakes

Prepare seitan according to manufacturer's directions. Set aside. In a small bowl, combine cream and stevia. Set aside. Melt butter in a large sauce pan. Sauté onions in butter until clear. Add prepared seitan, and cook for 5 minutes stirring frequently. In a large bowl, combine seitan mixture with stevia-cream mixture, eggs, parsley, dry mustard, paprika, salt, pepper, and chopped apple. Slowly stir in bread crumbs until texture is moist but firm. Shape into small cakes, and coat lightly with flour. Heat a small amount of oil in a frying pan. Fry each side until golden brown. Serve hot with Cocktail Sauce or Tangy Catsup (see index).

Makes 10 medium cakes.

---

*Seitan is a high protein food made with wheat gluten and is available at health food stores.

Southwest Peppers

1 pound chicken substitute
1 teaspoon salt
3 each green bell peppers, sliced
3 each red bell peppers, sliced
1/2 cup Italian Dressing (see index)
1/4 cup lime juice

1 teaspoon stevia blend *or*
   1/8 tsp. stevioside
1 1/2 teaspoon cumin
1 each onion, sliced
1/4 cup water
olive oil for browning

Blend Italian dressing, lime juice, stevia blend, and cumin together for a marinade. Add chicken substitute to the marinade. Marinate in refrigerator for at least 1 hour.

Pour 1/4 cup of water into a skillet. Bring to a boil; add sliced peppers and onions. Salt to taste. Cover, cook for 3 minutes, and then remove lid; continue cooking, stirring constantly, till water cooks off. Vegetables should be tender but crisp. Place peppers and onions on serving plates. Heat olive oil in a skillet over medium heat. Add chicken substitute, and sauté until golden brown. Add marinade and, stirring frequently, allow to cook down. Serve over peppers and onions.

Serves 4.

Spinach and Cheese Quiche

½ cup melted butter
10 each eggs
½ cup sifted flour
1 teaspoon baking powder
1 teaspoon salt
1 (10-oz) package frozen chopped
   spinach, thawed and squeezed
   very dry between towels

1 pint fine curd cottage cheese
½ pound grated sharp cheddar
   cheese
½ pound grated Monterey Jack
   cheese
1 teaspoon stevia blend *or*
   ⅛ tsp. stevioside

Beat eggs and stevia in large bowl. Mix in flour, baking powder, and salt. Stir in spinach. Add melted butter and cheeses, stirring till well mixed. Pour into greased 13 x 9 x 2-inch pan. Bake for 15 minutes at 400°F. Reduce heat to 340°F, and bake an additional 35 to 40 minutes.

Serves 12.

Pasta With Tofu

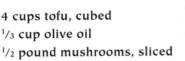

4 cups tofu, cubed
$^1/_3$ cup olive oil
$^1/_2$ pound mushrooms, sliced
1 small onion, finely chopped
1 tablespoon Italian seasoning

1 pound pasta, cooked as directed
28 ounces tomatoes, diced
2 teaspoons stevia blend *or*
    $^1/_4$ tsp. stevioside
Parmesan cheese for garnish

Sauté onions and mushrooms in a large skillet with butter until onions are clear. Add tofu and Italian seasoning. Stir in tomatoes and stevia. Simmer for 15 minutes stirring occasionally. Combine sauce with pasta and serve with fresh, grated Parmesan cheese.

Serves 4.

CHAPTER 10

Cakes & Cookies

CAKES AND COOKIES

Lemon Squares

CREAM CHEESE TOPPING MAKE THESE IRRESISTIBLE TREATS.

Filling:

2 each eggs

9 teaspoons stevia blend *or*
  1 tsp. stevioside

3 tablespoons lemon juice

1 teaspoon lemon flavoring

4 tablespoons butter, melted, cooled

1 tablespoon grated lemon rind

Crust:

5 tablespoons butter

1 tablespoon stevia blend

1 cup flour

Topping

4 ounces cream cheese, softened

4 ounces sour cream

1 teaspoon vanilla

1 teaspoon stevia blend or

$1/16$ teaspoon stevioside

For Crust:

In a bowl, beat butter and stevia till fluffy. Beat in 1 cup of flour till mixture resembles course crumbs. Press into the bottom of an ungreased 8 x 8 x 2-inch baking pan. Bake in a 350°F oven for 15 minutes or till golden.

Topping:

Wisk all ingredients together in bowl. Set aside.

Filling:

Beat eggs and stevia; mix in lemon juice, lemon extract, butter, and lemon rind. Pour mixture into hot baked crust. Bake at 350°F until lemon filling is set (about 20 minutes). While still hot, spread with cream cheese topping. Allow to cool, cut into squares.

Makes 20.

Any Fruit Bars

2 cups flour
3 teaspoons stevia blend *or* 3/8
   tsp. stevioside
¹/₄ teaspoon salt
¹/₂ cup margarine, cut into pieces

1 teaspoon vanilla
1 each egg
1 tablespoon skim milk
1 cup spreadable fruit

Combine flour, stevia, and salt in medium bowl. Cut in margarine until mixture resembles coarse crumbs. Mix in egg, milk, and vanilla. Press mixture into bottom of greased 11 x 7-inch baking dish. Bake in preheated 400°F oven until edges of crust are browned, about 15 minutes. Cool on wire rack. Spread spreadable fruit over cooled crust. Bake in preheated 400°F oven about 10 minutes. Cool on wire rack; cut into squares.

Makes about 2 dozen bars.

Cakes & Cookies

Chewy Coconut Bars

2 each eggs
10 teaspoons stevia blend *or*
   1 ¼ tsp. stevioside
¼ teaspoon maple flavoring
½ cup butter, melted
1 teaspoon vanilla
½ cup flour

1 teaspoon baking powder
¼ teaspoon salt
1 cup unsweetened shredded
   coconut*
½ cup chopped walnuts (optional)
½ cup raisins (optional)

In a bowl, combine flour, baking powder, salt, and stevia. Blend well.
Beat in eggs, maple flavoring, butter, and vanilla. Add remaining
ingredients; mix till well blended. Spread batter evenly in greased 8-
inch square baking pan. Bake 350°F for 15–20 minutes or till golden.

Makes 16 bars.

---

* Unsweetened coconut is available at health food stores

Chocolate Cake Brownies

FAST AND EASY

3 tablespoons stevia blend
$^1/_2$ cup apricot spreadable fruit or
   sugar-free jam (see index)
$^3/_4$ cup butter, softened
$^1/_2$ cup cocoa powder
2 each eggs
1 teaspoon vanilla

1 $^1/_2$ cups flour
1 teaspoon baking powder
$^1/_4$ teaspoon baking soda
$^1/_2$ cup milk
1 cup chopped nuts (optional)
Chocolate Cream Cheese Frosting
   (see index)

In a bowl, combine cocoa, flour, baking powder, baking soda, and stevia. Mix in spreadable fruit or sugar-free jam, eggs, vanilla, butter and milk. Beat till well combined. Fold in nuts. Pour batter into a greased 15 x 10 x 1-inch baking pan. Bake in a preheated 350°F oven 20–25 minutes or till a toothpick inserted near the center comes out clean. Cool in pan. Frost with Chocolate Cream Cheese Frosting. Cut into bars.

Makes 36.

Double Fudge Brownies

6 tablespoons margarine

4 ounces unsweetened baking chocolate

1/3 cup skim milk

1/3 cup unsweetened applesauce

1 each egg yolk

1 teaspoon vanilla

2/3 cup flour

4 tablespoons stevia blend *or* 1 1/2 tsp. stevioside

1/2 teaspoon baking powder

1/8 teaspoon salt

4 each egg whites

1/8 teaspoon cream of tartar

1/3 cup walnuts, chopped

Melt margarine and chocolate into milk and applesauce in a saucepan. Whisk mixture until chocolate is melted. Remove from heat and whisk in egg yolk, vanilla, and stevia until stevia is dissolved. Taste mixture and adjust sweetness to personal tastes by whisking in more stevia a little bit at a time until it dissolves. Mix in flour, baking powder, and salt until smooth. Allow to cool. Beat egg whites and cream of tartar until stiff peaks form. Fold in chocolate mixture. Fold in walnuts if desired. Pour batter into a greased 8-inch square baking pan. Bake in preheated oven at 350°F until brownies spring back from a light touch or a toothpick inserted near the center comes out clean (18–20 minutes). Cool on wire rack.

Makes 8 brownies.

Cappuccino Fudge Brownies

6 tablespoons butter

1 tablespoons instant coffee
  crystals

3 tablespoons cocoa

3 tablespoons stevia blend *or*
  1 tsp. stevioside

$^1/_3$ cup skim milk

$^1/_3$ cup unsweetened applesauce

1 each egg yolk

1 teaspoon vanilla

$^2/_3$ cup flour

$^1/_2$ teaspoon baking powder

$^1/_8$ teaspoon salt

4 each egg whites

$^1/_8$ teaspoon cream of tartar

$^1/_3$ cup walnuts, chopped

In a heavy saucepan, combine margarine, stevia, instant coffee crystals, cocoa, milk, and applesauce. Heat until margarine melts, then whisk mixture until stevia dissolves. Remove from heat and whisk in egg yolk and vanilla. Taste mixture and adjust sweetness to personal tastes, if necessary, by whisking in more stevia a tiny bit at a time till it dissolves. Mix in flour, baking powder, and salt until smooth. Allow to cool.

In a large mixing bowl, beat egg whites and cream of tartar until stiff peaks are formed. Fold in chocolate mixture and walnuts. Pour batter into a greased 8-inch square baking pan. Bake in preheated oven at 350°F until brownies bounce back after light touch or a toothpick inserted near the center comes out clean (18–20 minutes). Cut into squares.

Makes 16 brownies.

Buttery Shortbread Cookies

1 ¼ cups flour
2 ½ teaspoons stevia blend *or*
   ⁵/₁₆ tsp. stevioside

¼ teaspoon salt
½ cup butter

In a mixing bowl, combine flour, salt, and stevia. Cut in butter till mixture resembles fine crumbs and starts to cling. Form the mixture into a ball; knead till smooth. On an ungreased cookie sheet, pat or roll the dough into an 8-inch circle. Using your fingers, press to make a scalloped edge. With a knife, cut circle into 16 pie-shaped wedges, leaving wedges in the circle shape. Bake in a 325°F oven for 25–30 minutes or till bottom just starts to brown and center is set. While warm, cut circle into wedges again. Cool on the cookie sheet for 5 minutes. Remove from cookie sheet; cool on a wire rack.

Makes 16 wedges.

Pecan Sandies

THESE SCRUMPTIOUS COOKIES WILL BE A HIT AT ANY PARTY.

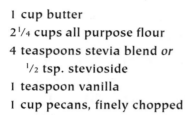

1 cup butter
2¼ cups all purpose flour
4 teaspoons stevia blend *or*
    ½ tsp. stevioside
1 teaspoon vanilla
1 cup pecans, finely chopped

Coating:

1 cup finely chopped pecans
1 teaspoon stevia blend *or*
    ⅛ tsp. stevioside

In a mixing bowl, beat butter with an electric mixer on medium to high speed for 30 seconds. Add about half of the flour, 4 teaspoons stevia blend, vanilla, and 1 tablespoon water. Beat till thoroughly combined. Beat in remaining flour. Stir in 1 cup of finely chopped pecans. In a separate bowl, combine 1 cup finely chopped pecans with 1 teaspoon stevia. Shape dough into crescents, 1-inch balls or 2-inch fingers. Press into pecan mixture covering the cookies completely. Place on an ungreased cookie sheet. Bake in a 325°F oven about 20 minutes or till bottoms are lightly browned. Cool cookies on a wire rack.

Makes about 3 dozen cookies.

Cream Cheese Cookies

YOU CAN MAKE FUN SHAPE WITH THESE COOKIES.

1/2 cup butter
1 3-oz. package cream cheese,
   softened
2 cups flour
1 each egg

1/2 teaspoon baking powder
1/2 teaspoon vanilla
3 1/2 tablespoons stevia blend *or*
   3/4 tsp. stevioside

Beat stevia, vanilla, butter, cream cheese, and egg in a bowl till fluffy. Add dry ingredients. Choose one of the following methods to shape cookies:

Method 1: Shape dough into 1-inch balls. Place 2 inches apart on greased cookie sheet. Using the bottom of a drinking glass press balls flat.

Method 2: Chill dough, roll out, and cut into desired shapes.

Bake in a preheated oven at 375°F for 8–10 minutes. Cool on a wire rack.

Makes about 60 cookies.

Variation:

Chocolate Cream Cheese Cookies: Prepare as above, except in a double boiler combine 2 ounces unsweetened bakers chocolate and 1 tablespoon stevia blend. Stir over medium heat till smooth. Add chocolate mixture to cream cheese.

Fruity Cookies

A LOVELY SURPRISE INSIDE EACH COOKIE.

1 cup margarine, softened
1 8-oz. package cream cheese, softened
3 teaspoons stevia blend *or* ³/₈ tsp. stevioside

2 cups flour
¹/₄ teaspoon salt
¹/₄ cup spreadable fruit or sugar-free jam

Beat margarine, cream cheese, and stevia until fluffy; mix in flour and salt to form a soft dough. Cover, and refrigerate until dough is firm. Roll dough on lightly floured surface into circles ¹/₈ inch thick; cut into 3-inch circles. Place ¹/₄ teaspoon of spreadable fruit in center of each round; fold rounds into halves. Seal edges with a fork. Pierce tops of cookies with knife. Bake cookies on greased cookie sheets in 350°F oven until lightly browned (about 8–10 minutes). Cool on wire racks.

Makes about 3 dozen.

Meringue Cookie Treats

**CONTAINS 0 FAT AND LOW CARBOHYDRATES –
THAT'S A TREAT!**

2 tablespoons nonfat powdered
   milk
3 teaspoons stevia blend *or*
   ³/₈ tsp. stevioside

2 each egg whites, at room
   temperature
¹/₄ teaspoon cream of tartar
¹/₄ teaspoon vanilla, to taste

Mix dry ingredients together. In a separate bowl, beat egg whites.
While beating, slowly add the dry ingredients. Beat until mixture is
super-stiff. This can take up to 10 minutes. You can not over-beat egg
whites. Add vanilla and mix just until blended. Place small, half-
teaspoon-size drops on oiled parchment paper. You can use a pastry
bag to make the drops. Bake in preheated oven at 350°F until dry all
the way through and slightly golden (about 25 minutes). Remove from
oven, and allow to cool. Store in an airtight container.

Makes about 45 cookies.

Peanut Butter Cookies

½ cup butter
¾ cup creamy natural peanut
   butter
2 tablespoons stevia blend *or*
   ¼ tsp. stevioside
¼ cup milk
1 each egg

1 teaspoon vanilla extract
1½ cups flour
1 teaspoon baking soda
½ teaspoon baking powder
½ teaspoon vanilla
¾ cup chopped roasted peanuts
   (optional)

In a small bowl, combine stevia, flour, baking soda, and baking powder; mix well. In another bowl, combine butter and peanut butter; beat till fluffy. Beat egg, milk, and vanilla into peanut butter mixture. Slowly add dry ingredients to wet ingredients. Beat till thoroughly combined. Shape dough into 1-inch balls. Place 2 inches apart on an ungreased cookie sheet. Flatten by crisscrossing with the tines of a fork. Bake in a 375°F oven for 7 to 9 minutes or till bottoms are lightly browned. Cool cookies on a wire rack.

Makes about 36.

Pumpkin Spice Cookies

MOIST AND CHEWY PERFECTLY SPICED COOKIES.

1/2 cup margarine, softened	1 1/2 teaspoons ground cinnamon
7 teaspoons stevia blend *or*	1/2 teaspoon ground cloves
7/8 tsp. stevioside	1/2 teaspoon ground nutmeg
1 cup canned pumpkin	1/8 teaspoon ground ginger
2 cups all purpose flour	1/2 cup sour cream
1 teaspoon baking soda	1/2 cup raisins, finely chopped
1/4 teaspoon salt	

Beat margarine and stevia until fluffy in large bowl; beat in pumpkin. Mix in flour, baking soda, salt, and spices alternately with sour cream. Mix in raisins. Spoon batter by heaping teaspoons onto greased cookie sheets. Bake cookies in preheated 375°F oven until browned (10 to 12 minutes).

Makes 6 dozen cookies.

Angle Food Cake

11 large egg whites, at room temperature

3 tablespoons stevia blend *or* 1 tsp. stevioside

1 cup cake flour

2 tablespoons stevia blend *or* ³/₄ tsp. stevioside

1 ½ teaspoons cream of tartar

1 teaspoon vanilla

Sift 2 tablespoons stevia blend and flour together. Set aside. In a large bowl, beat egg whites, cream of tartar, and 3 tablespoons stevia blend till stiff peaks form. Slowly sift about one-third flour mixture over stiff egg whites; fold in. Continue sifting and folding remaining flour mixture. Pour into an ungreased, 10-inch tube pan. Bake at 350°F for 40 to 45 minutes or till top springs back from a light touch. Immediately invert cake – leave in pan. This helps prevent the cake from falling. Allow to cool completely. Loosen sides of cake from pan with a knife; remove cake.

Makes 12 servings.

Hot-Milk Cake

1 cup cake flour
1 teaspoon baking powder
$^1/_2$ teaspoon baking soda
2 each eggs

5 teaspoons stevia blend *or*
  $^5/_8$ tsp. stevioside
$^1/_2$ cup milk
2 teaspoons margarine

In a small bowl, combine flour and baking powder. In another bowl, beat eggs with an electric mixer on high speed about 4 minutes. Gradually add stevia; beat at medium speed for 4 to 5 minutes or till light and fluffy. Add flour mixture; beat at low-to-medium speed just till combined.

In a saucepan, stirring constantly, heat margarine till it melts; add to batter, beating till combined. Pour into a greased 9 x 9 x 2-inch baking pan. Bake in a 350°F oven for 20 to 25 minutes or till a toothpick comes out clean.

Makes 9 servings.

Lemon Cake

¹/₄ cup margarine
2¹/₂ teaspoons stevia blend *or*
  ⁵/₁₆ tsp. stevioside
1 each egg

1 cup cake flour
1¹/₂ teaspoons baking powder
¹/₂ cup nonfat sour cream
5 teaspoons lemon juice

Cream butter with stevia blend and egg until fluffy. In a separate bowl, stir together flour, baking powder, and baking soda. In another bowl, combine sour cream with lemon juice. Add dry ingredients to creamed mixture alternately with liquid ingredients. Pour batter into a greased and floured, 9-inch cake pan. Bake in a preheated 350°F oven until golden and a toothpick inserted in the center comes out clean (about 25 minutes).

Makes 6 servings.

Lemon-Orange Sponge Cake

6 each egg yolks
½ cup sour cream
1 teaspoon orange extract
1 teaspoon lemon juice
1 teaspoon vanilla
5 teaspoons stevia blend *or*
⅝ tsp. stevioside

1 ¼ cups cake flour
6 each egg whites
½ teaspoon cream of tartar
2 teaspoons stevia blend *or*
¼ tsp. stevioside

In a bowl, beat stevia blend, egg yolks, sour cream, orange extract, lemon extract, and vanilla with an electric mixer on high until well mixed and fluffy. Slowly beat in the flour. Set the yolk mixture aside. Wash beaters. In a large bowl, beat egg whites, and cream of tartar at medium speed until soft peaks form. Sprinkle 2 teaspoons of stevia blend over the egg whites. Beat at high speed until stiff peaks form. Fold 1 cup of the beaten egg white mixture into the yolk mixture; fold yolk mixture into remaining white mixture. Pour into an ungreased, 10-inch tube pan. Bake in a 325°F oven for 55–65 minutes or till golden brown. Leaving cake in pan, quickly invert cake. This is to prevent the cake from falling. Cool thoroughly. Use a knife to loosen sides of cake from pan; remove cake from pan.

Makes 12 servings.

Pineapple Upside-Down Cake

1 14-oz. can unsweetened
  crushed pineapple in juice,
  undrained
2¹/₂ teaspoons lemon juice
2 teaspoons stevia blend *or*
  ¹/₄ tsp. stevioside
1¹/₂ teaspoons cornstarch
4 teaspoons margarine, at room
  temperature
2 teaspoons stevia blend *or*
  ¹/₄ tsp. stevioside

1 each egg
1 cup cake flour
1 teaspoon baking soda
¹/₄ teaspoon cinnamon
¹/₄ teaspoon nutmeg
¹/₄ teaspoon ginger
1 teaspoon vanilla
¹/₄ cup buttermilk

Drain pineapple, saving ¹/₂ cup juice. Mix pineapple, 1 teaspoon lemon juice, stevia blend, and cornstarch. Spread mixture evenly in the bottom of an 8-inch, square cake pan. Next, beat margarine and stevia blend in medium bowl until fluffy; beat in egg. In small bowl, combine flour, baking powder, baking soda, and spices. Combine ¹/₂ cup pineapple juice and remaining 1 teaspoon lemon juice; add to margarine mixture alternating with buttermilk. Spread batter over pineapple mixture in cake pan. Bake in preheated 350°F oven until browned and toothpick inserted in center comes out clean (about 25 minutes). Invert cake immediately onto serving plate.

Makes 8 servings.

Strawberry Shortcake

6 cups sliced strawberries
2 tablespoons stevia blend *or*
   ³/₄ tsp. stevioside
2 cups flour
2 teaspoons baking powder
2 tablespoons stevia blend *or*
   ³/₄ tsp. stevioside

¹/₂ cup butter
1 each egg, beaten
²/₃ cup milk
Whipped Cream (see index)

In a medium bowl, stir together strawberries and 2 tablespoons stevia blend. Set aside. In another bowl, stir together 2 tablespoons stevia blend, flour, and baking powder. Cut in margarine; add egg and milk. Stir just until moist. Spread into a greased 8 x 1¹/₂-inch round, baking pan. Bake at 450°F for 15 to 20 minutes or till toothpick inserted in center comes out clean. Cool in pan. Remove from pan. Divide into 2 layers. Spoon the strawberry mixture between layers and over top. Top with Whipped Cream. Serve immediately.

Makes 8 servings.

Cinnamon Swirl Coffee Cake

4 tablespoons margarine, softened
8 teaspoons stevia blend *or*
   1 tsp. stevioside
1 each egg
1/4 cup sour cream
2 teaspoons maple flavoring

2³/4 cups cake flour
4 teaspoons baking powder
1/2 teaspoon salt
1 cup skim milk
1 1/2 teaspoons ground cinnamon

Beat margarine and stevia blend until fluffy in medium bowl. Beat in egg, sour cream, and maple flavoring. In a separate bowl, combine flour, baking powder, and salt. Alternating with milk, beat flour mixture into margarine mixture. Spread 1/3 of the batter into a greased and floured bundt pan. Sprinkle with 1/2 of the cinnamon. Repeat layers, ending with cake batter. Bake cake in preheated 375°F oven for 25–30 minutes or till toothpick inserted in center of cake comes out clean. Cool cake in the pan for 5 minutes; remove from pan and cool on wire rack.

Makes 8 servings

Chocolate Raspberry Cake

SURE TO BE A FAMILY FAVORITE.

4 teaspoons margarine, softened
$^1/_4$ cup raspberry spreadable fruit
1 each egg
5 teaspoons stevia blend *or*
   $^5/_8$ tsp. stevioside
3 teaspoons Dutch cocoa
1 ounce unsweetened baking
   chocolate

$^1/_2$ cup milk
1 cup flour
1 teaspoon baking powder
$^1/_2$ teaspoon baking soda
$^1/_4$ teaspoon salt

In a double boiler, combine Dutch cocoa, baking chocolate, and milk. Over medium heat, stir until smooth.

Beat margarine, preserves, egg, and stevia in medium bowl till smooth. In another bowl, combine flour, baking powder, baking soda, and salt. Mix dry ingredients into preserve mixture alternately with melted chocolate mixture. Pour batter into greased and floured, 8-inch cake pan. Bake in 350°F oven until toothpick inserted in center of cake comes out clean (about 20 minutes). Cool in pan 5 minutes; remove from pan and cool completely.

Makes 8 servings.

Dark Chocolate Bar Cake

A CHOCOHOLIC'S DREAM!

6 tablespoons margarine
5 1/2 tablespoons stevia blend *or*
   11/16 tsp. stevioside
4 ounces unsweetened chocolate
1/3 cup skim milk
1/3 cup apricot sugar-free
   preserves
3 each egg whites

1/8 teaspoon cream of tartar
1/4 cup flour
1/8 teaspoon salt
1 each egg yolk
1 teaspoon vanilla
Chocolate Glaze (optional, see
   index)

Heat margarine, chocolate, milk, and apricot preserves, in small saucepan, stirring frequently, until chocolate is almost melted. Remove pan from heat; continue stirring until chocolate is melted and mixture is smooth. Briskly stir in egg yolk, vanilla, and stevia.

Beat egg whites and cream of tartar to stiff peaks in large bowl. Fold chocolate mixture into egg whites. Combine flour and salt and fold into egg whites. Lightly grease bottom of 9-inch, round cake pan and line with wax paper. Pour cake batter into pan. Bake in preheated 350°F oven for 18–20 minutes till cake is just firm when lightly touched. (Do not over bake). Using a sharp knife, loosen the sides of the cake from the pan. This will help keep cake from cracking as it cools. Cool cake completely in pan on wire rack; refrigerate until chilled (1 to 2 hours). Remove cake from pan, and place on serving plate. Spread with Chocolate Glaze, if desired.

Makes 12 servings.

Cakes & Cookies

Moist and Lite
Chocolate Cupcakes

LOW-FAT CHOCOLATE TREATS.

1 cup flour
5 teaspoons stevia blend *or*
   ⁵/₈ tsp. stevioside
2 teaspoons cocoa
1 teaspoon baking soda

1 teaspoon baking powder
¹/₂ cup light salad dressing
¹/₂ cup water
1 teaspoon vanilla

In a large bowl, combine flour, stevia, cocoa, and baking soda. In a small bowl, stir together salad dressing, water, and vanilla until well blended. Stir wet ingredients into dry ingredients until just mixed. Spoon into medium, greased muffin cups. Bake in 350°F oven for 12 minutes or until toothpick inserted in center comes out clean.

Makes 12 medium cupcakes.

Chocolate Cheesecake

Graham Cracker Crust:

1 ¼ cups graham cracker crumbs
4 tablespoons margarine, melted
1 teaspoon stevia blend *or*
    ⅛ tsp. stevioside
or Pretzel Crust (see index)

Cheesecake:

3 8-oz. packages cream cheese,
    softened
8 ½ teaspoons stevia blend *or*
    1 tsp. stevioside
3 each eggs
2 tablespoons cornstarch
1 cup sour cream
⅓ cup Dutch-process cocoa
1 teaspoon vanilla

Crust:

Mix graham cracker crumbs, margarine, and stevia in bottom of 9-inch springform pan. Pat graham cracker mixture evenly on bottom and ½ inch up side of pan.

Cheesecake:

Beat cream cheese and stevia in large bowl until fluffy; beat in eggs, and cornstarch. Mix in sour cream, cocoa, and vanilla until well blended. Pour mixture onto crust.

Place cheesecake in roasting pan on oven rack; add 1 inch of water to roasting pan. Bake cheesecake at 300°F for 45 to 50 minutes; just until set in the center. Turn oven off; remove cheesecake from roasting pan; return cheesecake to oven and let cheesecake cool 3 hours in oven with door slightly open. Refrigerate at least 8 hours. Remove cheesecake from pan. Place on serving plate.

Makes 16 servings.

New York Style Cheesecake

12 teaspoons stevia blend *or*
  1 ¹/₂ tsp. stevioside
2 each eggs
2 each egg whites
2 tablespoons cornstarch

3 8-oz. packages cream cheese,
  softened
1 cup sour cream
1 teaspoon vanilla
Pretzel Crust (see index)

In a bowl, beat cream cheese and stevia until fluffy. Beat in egg whites, eggs, and cornstarch. Beat in vanilla and sour cream. Pour mixture over crust in a springform pan. Bake in a preheated oven at 300°F until firm in center (approx. 45–60 minutes). Turn off oven and let cheesecake cool. Refrigerate overnight. Serve with fresh fruit or a sauce if desired (see *Desert Sauces*).

Makes 16 servings.

Pumpkin Cheesecake
With Sour Cream Topping

24 ounces cream cheese
3 teaspoons stevia blend *or*
   ³/₈ tsp. stevioside
2 each eggs
15 ounces pumpkin
²/₃ cup evaporated milk
2 tablespoons cornstarch
1 ¹/₄ teaspoons ground cinnamon
¹/₂ teaspoon nutmeg

Topping:

2 cups sour cream
2 teaspoons stevia blend *or*
   ¹/₄ tsp. stevioside
1 teaspoon vanilla
Pretzel Crust (see index)

Beat cream cheese and stevia in a large bowl until fluffy. Beat in eggs, pumpkin, and evaporated milk. Add cornstarch and spices. Beat well, and pour into crust. Bake at 350°F for 55 to 60 minutes until center is set.

Topping:

Combine sour cream, stevia blend, and vanilla in a bowl and mix well.

Spread topping over surface of warm cheesecake and allow to cool on a wire rack. Chill for several hours or overnight.

Makes 16 servings.

Cakes & Cookies

CHAPTER 11

Pies & Pastries

PIES & PASTRIES

Apple Pie – 145

Banana Cream Pie – 147

Cheese Pastry – 157

Cherry Pie – 146

Chocolate Cookie Crust – 160

Chocolate Cream Pie – 148

Coconut Crust – 161

Coconut Custard Pie – 150

Cookie Crust – 160

Double-Crust Pastry – 157

Grape-Nuts® Crust – 161

Key Lime Pie – 152

Lemon Meringue Pie – 151

Meringue for Pie – 156

Nutty Coconut Cream Pie – 149

Oil Pastry – 159

Orange Cookie Crust – 160

Pretzel Crust – 162

Pumpkin Pie – 156

Rich Pastry – 159

Single-Crust Pastry – 158

Sour Cream and Raisin Pie – 155

Strawberry Chiffon Pie – 154

Strawberry Cream Cheese Pie – 153

Vanilla Cream Pie – 147

Apple Pie

6–8 each tart apples, peeled and thinly sliced
3 teaspoons stevia blend *or* ³/₈ tsp. stevioside
3 tablespoons all-purpose flour
1 tablespoon cinnamon
1 dash ground nutmeg
2 tablespoons butter
1 tablespoon lemon juice
1 dash salt
Double-Crust Pastry (see index)

In a mixing bowl, combine stevia blend, lemon juice, flour, and spices. Add apples; toss to coat fruit. Prepare Double-Crust Pastry. Place bottom pastry in a 9-inch pie plate. Place apple pie filling in pastry. Carefully position top crust. Seal and flute edge. Cover edge with foil. Bake in a 375°F oven for 25 minutes. Remove foil. Bake for 20 to 25 minutes more till the top is golden and fruit is tender.

Serves 8.

Cherry Pie

2 16-oz packages frozen, no-
　sugar-added, pitted cherries
3/4 cup reserved cherry juice
5 tablespoons stevia blend *or*
　1 3/4 tsp. stevioside

4 teaspoons all-purpose flour
4 teaspoons cornstarch
1/4 teaspoon ground nutmeg
1 teaspoon almond extract
Double-Crust Pastry (see index)

Thaw cherries completely in a strainer placed in a bowl; reserve 3/4 cup cherry juice. Set aside. In small, heavy saucepan, mix stevia, flour, cornstarch, and nutmeg. Stirring constantly, add cherry juice and heat to boiling. Continue stirring and cooking 2 more minutes. Remove from heat; stir in cherries and almond extract. Roll half of pastry on floured surface into circle 1 inch larger than inverted 9-inch pie pan. Place pastry into pan. Pour cherry mixture into pastry. Roll remaining pastry on floured surface to 1/8-inch thickness. Cut into 10 strips, 1/2-inch wide. Arrange pastry strips over filling. Weave into lattice design; trim. Fold edge of lower crust over ends of lattice strips. Seal and flute edge. Bake at 425°F for 35 to 40 minutes or till pastry is browned. Cool.

Makes 8 servings.

Vanilla Cream Pie

9 teaspoons stevia blend *or*
  1 ¹/₈ tsp. stevioside
¹/₄ cup cornstarch
2 tablespoons butter
3 cups milk
4 each egg yolks, beaten

2 teaspoons vanilla
baked Single-Crust Pastry (see
  index)
Meringue for Pie or Whipped
  Cream (see index)

Combine stevia, cornstarch, and milk in a saucepan. Stirring constantly, cook over medium heat till mixture is thick and bubbly. Reduce heat, add 1 tablespoon butter, and continue cooking and stirring for 3 more minutes. Stir 1 cup of hot mixture into beaten egg yolks. Stirring constantly, add all of egg mixture to the hot mixture in the saucepan. Still stirring constantly, cook over medium heat till near boiling. Continue cooking and stirring for 3 more minutes. Remove from heat. Stir in butter and vanilla. Pour the hot filling into baked crust.

Makes 8 servings.

Variations:

Banana Cream Pie: Prepare as above, but slice 2 medium bananas into the bottom of the baked crust. Pour filling over bananas.

Whipped Cream Topping: Prepare as above, chill hot pie, and then spread whipped cream over filling.

Meringue Topping: Prepare as above, but spread meringue over hot filling, sealing edges. Bake at 350°F for 15 minutes or till golden. Cool.

Chocolate Cream Pie

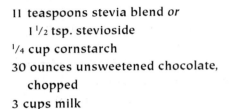

11 teaspoons stevia blend *or*
    1 ¹/₂ tsp. stevioside
¹/₄ cup cornstarch
30 ounces unsweetened chocolate,
    chopped
3 cups milk

4 each egg yolks, beaten
2 teaspoons vanilla
baked Single-Crust Pastry (see
    index)
Meringue or Whipped Cream (see
    index)

Combine stevia, cornstarch, and milk in a saucepan; add chopped chocolate. Stirring constantly, cook over medium heat till mixture is thick and bubbly. Reduce heat. Add 1 tablespoon butter; continue cooking and stirring for 3 more minutes. Stir 1 cup of hot mixture into beaten egg yolks. Stirring constantly, add all of egg mixture to the hot mixture in the saucepan. Cook over medium heat, still stirring con-stantly, till near boiling. Continue cooking and stirring for 3 more minutes. Remove from heat. Stir in butter and vanilla. Pour the hot filling into baked crust.

Makes 8 servings.

Variations:

Whipped Cream Topping: Chill hot pie then spread whipped cream over filling.

Meringue Topping: Prepare as above, but spread meringue over hot filling, sealing edges. Bake at 350°F for 15 minutes or till golden. Cool.

Nutty Coconut Cream Pie

9 teaspoons stevia blend *or*
   1 $^{1}/_{8}$ tsp. stevioside
$^{1}/_{3}$ cup cornstarch
2 tablespoons all-purpose flour
$^{1}/_{4}$ teaspoon salt
3 each eggs
3 cups milk
1 tablespoon butter
2 teaspoons vanilla extract
2 teaspoons almond extract

1 $^{1}/_{4}$ cups coconut flakes (sugar-
   free coconut is available at
   health food stores)
$^{3}/_{4}$ cup chopped toasted almonds
Whipped Cream (see index)
toasted coconut (optional)
prepared Coconut Crust (see
   index) or favorite single crust
   pastry

In medium saucepan, stir together stevia, cornstarch, flour, and salt; stir in eggs until mixture is well blended. Gradually stir in milk. Cook over medium heat, stirring constantly, until mixture boils; continue boiling and stirring 2 more minutes. Remove from heat. Stir in butter, almond extract and vanilla; stir in coconut and chopped almonds until blended. Pour into baked pie crust. Press plastic wrap directly onto surface; refrigerate 6 to 8 hours or until set. Just before serving, spread with Whipped Cream; sprinkle with toasted coconut.

Makes 8 servings.

Coconut Custard Pie

THIS BAKED PIE IS FAST AND EASY TO PREPARE.

4 each eggs
¹/₄ teaspoon salt
2 cups skim milk
8 teaspoons stevia blend *or*
   1 tsp. stevioside

2 teaspoons coconut extract
¹/₂ cup flaked coconut (or use
   sugar-free coconut meal,
available at health food stores)
Single-Crust Pastry (see index)

Beat eggs and salt in large bowl until thick and lemon-colored (about 5 minutes). Mix in milk and remaining ingredients. Pour mixture into pastry. Bake pie in preheated 425°F oven for 15 minutes. Reduce temperature to 350°F and bake 20–25 more minutes or till a knife inserted near center comes out clean. Refrigerate till chilled (about 2 hours).

Makes 8 servings.

Lemon Meringue Pie

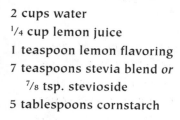

2 cups water
$^1/_4$ cup lemon juice
1 teaspoon lemon flavoring
7 teaspoons stevia blend *or*
   $^7/_8$ tsp. stevioside
5 tablespoons cornstarch

3 each eggs, beaten
1 teaspoon margarine
baked Single-Crust Pastry (see
   index)
Meringue (see index)

Mix water, lemon juice, stevia blend, and cornstarch in medium sauce-pan. Stirring constantly, heat to boiling; continue boiling and stirring 1 minute longer. Stir about 1 cup hot cornstarch mixture into the beaten eggs. Stirring constantly, add egg mixture to remaining hot cornstarch mixture; cook, still stirring constantly, over low heat for 5 minutes. Remove from heat; add margarine, stirring until melted. Pour mixture into baked pie shell.

Makes 8 servings.

Key Lime Pie

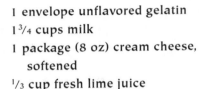

1 envelope unflavored gelatin
1 ³/₄ cups milk
1 package (8 oz) cream cheese,
 softened
¹/₃ cup fresh lime juice

6 teaspoons stevia blend *or*
 ³/₄ tsp. stevioside
baked 9-inch Cookie Crust (see
 index)

Sprinkle gelatin over ¹/₂ cup milk in small saucepan; let stand 2 to 3 minutes to soften. Stirring constantly, cook over low heat, until gelatin is dissolved. In a small bowl, beat cream cheese until fluffy; beat in remaining 1 ¹/₄ cups milk and gelatin mixture. Mix in lime juice and stevia. Poor filling into cooled crust. Refrigerate pie until set (about 2 hours).

Makes 8 servings.

Strawberry Cream Cheese Pie

1 8 oz. package cream cheese, softened
1 teaspoon vanilla
3 teaspoons stevia blend *or*
   $^3/_8$ tsp. stevioside
1 cup cold water
2 tablespoons cornstarch

1 package gelatin
6 teaspoons stevia blend *or*
   $^3/_4$ tsp. stevioside
1 pint strawberries, hulled, sliced
baked 9-inch Cookie Crust (see index)

Beat cream cheese, vanilla, and stevia in small bowl until fluffy; spread evenly in bottom of cooled crust. In small saucepan, mix cold water, 6 teaspoons stevia blend, and cornstarch; heat to boiling stirring constantly until thickened (about 2 minutes). Add gelatin, stirring until gelatin is dissolved. Cool 10 minutes. Arrange half of the sliced strawberries over the cream cheese. Spoon half the gelatin mixture over strawberries. Arrange remaining strawberries over pie and spoon remaining gelatin mixture over top. Refrigerate at least 2 hours or until pie is set and chilled.

Makes 8 servings.

Strawberry Chiffon Pie

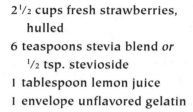

2 1/2 cups fresh strawberries, hulled
6 teaspoons stevia blend *or* 1/2 tsp. stevioside
1 tablespoon lemon juice
1 envelope unflavored gelatin
2/3 cup water
2 each egg whites
1/2 cup whipping cream
Cookie Crust (see index)
Whipped Cream, optional (see index)

Crush strawberries with a fork in a large mixing bowl. Stir in 2 teaspoons stevia blend *or* 1/2 teaspoon stevioside and lemon juice; set aside.

Stir together 2 teaspoons stevia blend *or* 1/2 teaspoon stevioside, 2/3 cup water, and the gelatin in a small saucepan. Allow to soften 2 minutes. Cook over low heat, stirring constantly, till gelatin dissolves. Remove from heat. Cool to room temperature. Pour the cooled gelatin mixture into the strawberry mixture. Mix well. Refrigerate to the consistency of corn syrup, stirring occasionally (about 1 hour). Do not overchill. Remove from refrigerator.

In a large bowl, beat the egg whites on high speed with an electric mixer till soft peaks form. Gradually add 2 teaspoons stevia blend *or* 1/2 teaspoon stevioside. Beat till stiff peaks form. Fold in chilled gelatin mixture. In a medium bowl, beat cream till soft peaks form. Fold whipped cream into strawberry mixture. Chill about 1 hour. Spoon filling into cooled Cookie Crust. Chill pie at least 6 hours or till set.

Makes 8 servings.

Sour Cream and Raisin Pie

9 teaspoons stevia blend *or*
  1 $^1/_8$ tsp. stevioside
$^1/_3$ cup cornstarch
3 cups milk
4 each egg yolks, beaten
1 tablespoon butter

2 teaspoons vanilla
1 cup raisins
$^1/_2$ cup sour cream
baked Single-Crust Pastry (see index)
Whipped Cream (see index)

Combine stevia, cornstarch, and milk in a saucepan. Stirring continuously, cook over medium heat till mixture is thick and bubbly. Reduce heat; continue cooking and stirring for 3 more minutes. Stir 1 cup of hot mixture into beaten egg yolks. Stirring constantly, add all of egg mixture to the hot mixture in the saucepan. Cook, stirring constantly, over medium heat till near boiling. Continue cooking and stirring for 3 more minutes. Remove from heat. Stir in raisins, sour cream, butter, and vanilla. Pour the hot filling into baked crust. Chill. Spread whipped cream over pie. Serve cold.

Makes 8 servings.

Pumpkin Pie

GUESTS WILL NEVER KNOW WHAT'S MISSING.

5 teaspoons stevia blend *or*
   $^5/_8$ tsp. stevioside
$^1/_2$ teaspoon salt
1 teaspoon ground cinnamon
$^1/_2$ teaspoon ginger

1/4 teaspoon allspice
2 each eggs
15 ounces pumpkin pie filling
1 $^1/_2$ cups evaporated milk
Single-Crust Pastry(see index)

In a large bowl, combine all ingredients. Mix until fluffy. Pour into pie crust. Bake at 350°F for 40 to 50 minutes or until a knife inserted into the center comes out clean. Allow to cool. Top with Whipped Cream (see index).

Makes 8 servings.

Meringue for Pie

4 each egg whites
$^1/_4$ teaspoon cream of tartar
$^1/_2$ teaspoon vanilla

3 teaspoons stevia blend *or*
   $^3/_8$ tsp. stevioside

Beat 4 egg whites and vanilla in medium bowl until foamy; add cream of tartar and beat to soft peaks. Gradually beat in 3 teaspoons stevia blend, beating to stiff peaks. Spread meringue over pie, carefully sealing edge of crust. Bake in a 350°F oven for 15 minutes or till golden.

Makes 8 servings.

Pies & Pastries

Double-Crust Pastry

2 cups all-purpose flour	2 teaspoons stevia blend *or*
1/2 teaspoon salt	1/4 tsp. stevioside
2/3 cup shortening	6–7 tablespoons water

Stir together flour, stevia, and salt in a mixing bowl. Cut in shortening till pieces are the size of small peas. Slowly add water, 1 tablespoon at a time, till dough is moist. Divide dough in half. Form each half into a ball. On a floured surface, flatten one ball of dough. Roll dough to form a circle about 1 inch larger than an inverted 9-inch pie plate. Wrap pastry around rolling pin. Unroll into a 9-inch pie plate. For top crust, roll remaining dough. Cut slits to let steam out.

Fill crust in pie plate with filling. Place top crust on filling. Trim crust 1/2 inch beyond plate. Flute edge. Bake as directed in individual recipes.

Variation:

Cheese Pastry: Prepare as above, adding 1 cup shredded cheddar cheese to flour. Perfect for apple pie.

Single-Crust Pastry

1 1/4 cups all-purpose flour
1/4 teaspoon salt
1/3 cup shortening

3–4 tablespoons water
2 teaspoons stevia blend *or*
  1/4 tsp. stevioside

Stir together flour, stevia, and salt in a mixing bowl. Cut in shortening till pieces are the size of small peas. Slowly add water, 1 tablespoon at a time, till dough is moist. Form into a ball. On a floured surface, flatten one ball of dough. Roll dough to form a circle about 1 inch larger than an inverted 9-inch pie plate. Wrap pastry around rolling pin. Unroll into a 9-inch pie plate. Trim to 1/2 inch beyond edge of pie plate; fold crust under. Flute edges. Bake as directed in recipes.

Baked Pastry Shell: Prepare as above; with a fork, prick bottom and sides of pastry. Bake at 450°F for 10 to 14 minutes or till golden. Cool.

Oil Pastry

THIS LIGHT AND FLAKY CRUST IS EASY TO MAKE.

$^1/_2$ cup milk
$^1/_2$ cup cooking oil
2 teaspoons stevia blend *or*
   1/4 tsp. stevioside

2 cups flour
salt to taste

In a mixing bowl, stir together flour and salt. Pour oil and milk into a measuring cup; add all at once to flour mixture. Stir with a fork. Form into 2 balls. Place each ball of dough between 2 squares of wax paper. Roll each ball into a circle. Peel off top paper and fit dough, paper side up, into 9-inch pie plates. Remove paper.

Makes one 9-inch double-crust pastry or two 9-inch single-crust pastries.

Rich Pastry

$^3/_4$ cup all-purpose flour
3 teaspoons stevia blend *or*
   $^3/_8$ tsp. stevioside
2$^1/_4$ teaspoons cornstarch

$^1/_8$ teaspoon salt
6 tablespoons margarine, cut into
   pieces
$^3/_4$ teaspoon vanilla

Combine flour, stevia blend, cornstarch, and salt in medium bowl; cut in margarine until mixture resembles coarse crumbs. Sprinkle with vanilla; mix with hands to form dough. Press dough evenly on bottom and $^1/_4$-inch up side of 8-inch, square baking pan. Bake in preheated 350°F oven until lightly browned (about 10 minutes). Cool on wire rack. *Makes 16 servings.*

Cookie Crust

½ cup butter
3 ounces cream cheese
2 cups flour
2 tablespoons stevia blend *or*
   ¼ tsp. stevioside

1 each egg
½ teaspoon baking powder
½ teaspoon vanilla

In a medium bowl, beat margarine, cream cheese, and stevia with an electric mixer on high speed till creamy. Add 1 cup of the flour, egg, baking powder, and vanilla. Beat till well blended. Mix in remaining flour. Cover; chill 1 hour. Roll into circle on wax paper. Invert over pie pan; shape edge. Bake in a 375°F oven about 12 minutes or till golden. Cool before filling. Use for chiffon, pudding, or ice-cream pies.

Makes one 9-inch, single-crust pastry.

Variations:

Chocolate Cookie Crust: Prepare as above, increasing stevia blend to 2½ tablespoons and adding 2 squares (2 ounces) unsweetened chocolate, melted and slightly cooled, with the butter and cream cheese mixture.

Orange Cookie Crust: Prepare as above, adding ½ teaspoon orange zest and 1 tablespoon frozen orange juice concentrate with the vanilla.

Coconut Crust

2 cups flaked coconut
2 teaspoons stevia blend *or*
   1/4 tsp. stevioside

3 tablespoons margarine or butter,
   melted

In a bowl, mix 2 cups flaked coconut with stevia. Next, add melted margarine or butter. Press firmly onto bottom and sides of a 9-inch pie plate. Bake in a 325°F oven for 20 minutes or till edge is golden. Cool before filling. Great for chiffon, ice-cream, or coconut pies.

Grape-Nuts® Crust

1 1/2 cups Grape-Nuts[a]
4 tablespoons margarine or butter

2 teaspoons stevia blend *or*
   1/4 tsp. stevioside
   1/2 teaspoon salt

Melt margarine and mix with **Grape-Nuts®**. Sprinkle stevia blend and salt over the mixture and mix well. Pack into a baking dish that will be used to bake the pie or cheesecake. Place in a preheated oven at 350°F for 8 minutes or until crust in lightly browned. Allow to cool before using with cheesecake or pie.

Pretzel Crust

1 ½ cups pretzels, crushed
4 tablespoons margarine or butter

2 teaspoons stevia blend *or*
¼ tsp. stevioside

Melt margarine and mix with crushed pretzels. Sprinkle stevia over the mixture and mix well. Pack into a baking dish that will be used to bake the pie or cheesecake. Place in a preheated oven at 350°F for 8 minutes or until crust is lightly browned. Allow to cool before using with cheesecake or pie.

CHAPTER 12

Desserts & Candies

DESSERTS & CANDIES

Almond Velvet Ice Cream – 180
Baked Apples – 172
Bread Pudding – 166
Cappuccino Ice Cream – 179
Chocolate Chips – 187
Chocolate Chocolate-Chip Ice Cream – 178
Chocolate Fudge Treats – 186
Chocolate Ice Cream – 178
Chocolate Mousse – 168
Chocolate Pudding – 167
Cream Puffs – 183
Creamy Frozen Pops – 181
Creamy Stirred Rice Pudding – 169
Dessert Crepes – 182
Dipping Chocolate – 187
Flan with Butterscotch Sauce – 171
Fresh Fruit Yogurt – 175
Fruit Juice Gelatin Blocks – 174
Fruity Gelatin – 175
Fudge Balls – 185
Light & Fluffy Tapioca – 170
Orange Frozen Yogurt – 180
Peach Cobbler – 173
Peanut Butter Balls – 184
Pina Colada Frozen Yogurt – 181
Poached Pears – 174
Powdered Sugar Replacement – 188
Sour Cream Vanilla Pudding – 165
Vanilla Ice Cream – 176
Vanilla Ice Milk – 177
Vanilla Pudding – 165
Yogurt with Fruit Preserves – 176

Vanilla Pudding

6 teaspoons stevia blend or
   3/4 tsp. stevioside
3 tablespoons cornstarch
3 cups milk

4 each eggs, beaten
1 tablespoon margarine
2 teaspoons vanilla

In a heavy medium saucepan, combine stevia blend and cornstarch. Stir in milk. Stirring constantly, cook over medium heat till mixture is thickened and bubbly. Continue cooking and stirring for 2 more minutes. Remove from heat. Gradually stir about 1 cup of the hot mixture into beaten eggs. Slowly stir all of the egg mixture into the remaining hot mixture in the saucepan. Cook till nearly bubbly, but do not boil. Reduce heat. Continue cooking and stirring 3 more minutes. Remove from heat. Stir in margarine and vanilla. Pour pudding into a bowl. Cover the surface with clear plastic wrap. Chill.

Makes 6 servings.

Variation:

Sour Cream Vanilla Pudding: Prepare as above. After chilling, stir in one 8-ounce carton dairy sour cream.

Bread Pudding

TRY THIS CLASSIC DESSERT FOR BREAKFAST.

4 beaten eggs
2 cups milk
8 teaspoons stevia blend *or*
   1 tsp. stevioside

1 teaspoon ground cinnamon
1 teaspoon vanilla
3 cups (4 slices) dry bread cubes
⅓ cup raisins, chopped

Place dry bread cubes in an 8 x 1½-inch baking dish. Sprinkle raisins over bread. In a medium mixing bowl, beat together eggs, milk, stevia, cinnamon, and vanilla. Pour egg mixture over the bread and raisins. Bake in a 325°F oven for 35–40 minutes or till a knife inserted near the center comes out clean. Cool slightly. Serve with Stirred Custard Sauce (see index).

Makes 6 servings.

Chocolate Pudding

9 teaspoons stevia blend *or*
   1 tsp. stevioside
$^1/_3$ cup cocoa powder
3 tablespoons cornstarch

3 cups milk
4 each egg yolks
1 tablespoon margarine
2 teaspoons vanilla

In a heavy saucepan, combine stevia, cornstarch, and cocoa. Add milk; stir well. Over medium heat, stirring constantly, cook till mixture is thickened and bubbly. Continue cooking and stirring for 1 minute more. Remove from heat. Stir about 1 cup of the hot milk mixture into the beaten egg yolks. Add all of the egg mixture to the remaining hot milk mixture in the saucepan. Stirring constantly, cook till nearly boiling. Do not boil, or mixture may curdle. Reduce heat; continue cooking and stirring 3 minutes more. Remove from heat. Stir in margarine and vanilla. Pour pudding into a bowl. Cover the surface with clear plastic wrap. Chill in refrigerator at least 2 hours before serving.

Makes 4 Servings

Chocolate Mousse

1 teaspoon (1 pkg.) gelatin
1 tablespoon cold water
1 tablespoon boiling water
6 teaspoons stevia blend *or*
   $^3/_4$ tsp. stevioside

$^1/_4$ cup cocoa powder
1 cup heavy whipping cream
1 teaspoon vanilla

In a small bowl, sprinkle gelatin over cold water; let stand 5 minutes to soften. Add boiling water, stirring until gelatin is completely dissolved and mixture is clear. Cool slightly. In medium bowl, stir together stevia and cocoa; add whipping cream and vanilla. Beat at medium speed, scraping bottom of bowl occasionally, until stiff peaks form. Pour in gelatin mixture and beat until well blended. Spoon into serving dishes. Chill about $^1/_2$ hour.

Makes 4 servings.

Variations: Add a dash of rum, Kahlua or instant coffee crystals while beating mixture.

Creamy Stirred Rice Pudding

3 cups milk
$^1/_3$ cup long grain rice
$^1/_3$ cup chopped raisins
$3^1/_2$ teaspoons stevia blend *or*
   $^7/_{16}$ tsp. stevioside

1 teaspoon vanilla
$^1/_2$ teaspoon ground nutmeg

In a heavy, medium saucepan, bring milk to boiling. Stir in uncooked rice and raisins. Cover; cook over low heat, stirring often, for 30 to 40 minutes or till most of the milk is absorbed. (Mixture may appear lumpy.) Stir in the stevia blend, vanilla, and nutmeg. Spoon into dessert dishes. Serve warm or cold.

Makes 6 servings.

Light & Fluffy Tapioca

1 each egg white	3 tablespoons minute tapioca
1 tablespoon nonfat dry milk powder	2 cups milk
3 teaspoons stevia blend *or* ³/₈ tsp. stevioside	1 each egg yolk
	1 ½ teaspoons vanilla

In a small bowl, mix 1 teaspoon stevia blend with 1 tablespoon of dry powdered milk; set aside. In another bowl, using an electric mixer on high speed, beat egg white until foamy. Gradually add powdered milk mixture to egg whites, beating until soft peaks form. Mix tapioca with remaining stevia blend, milk, and egg yolk in a medium saucepan. Let stand 5 minutes. Stirring constantly, cook on medium heat until mixture comes to a full boil. Remove from heat. Stir tapioca mixture into egg-white mixture until well blended. Stir in vanilla. Dispense into small dessert bowls. Cool.

Makes approximately 6 servings.

Flan with Butterscotch Sauce

1 quart skim milk
5 each eggs
7 teaspoons stevia blend *or*
   $^7/_8$ tsp. stevioside

2 teaspoons vanilla
Butterscotch Sauce (see index)

In a heavy saucepan, heat milk just to simmering. Beat eggs until foamy in medium bowl; gradually whisk hot milk into eggs. Stir in stevia and vanilla. Pour milk mixture through a strainer into an ungreased, 1-quart casserole or soufflé dish; cover with lid or aluminum foil. Place dish in roasting pan on middle rack of oven. Pour 2 inches of water into roasting pan. Bake at 325°F until custard is set and sharp knife inserted near the center comes out clean (1 to 1$^1/_4$ hours). Remove dish from roasting pan, and cool to room temperature on wire rack. Refrigerate until chilled (5 to 6 hours). Spoon custard into dishes; top with Butterscotch Sauce.

Makes 5 servings.

Baked Apples

4 each small apples
1 teaspoon butter or margarine
2 teaspoons stevia blend *or*
   $^1/_4$ tsp. stevioside

$^1/_3$ teaspoon cinnamon
$^1/_3$ cup apple juice or water
$^1/_2$ cup raisins or mixed dried fruit
   bits

Remove apple cores, leaving half an inch of core at bottom of each apple. Prick skins with fork; place apples in a 2-quart casserole. In a small saucepan, melt margarine. Stir in stevia, cinnamon, lemon juice, raisins, and walnuts. Spoon mixture into apple centers. Bake in a 350°F oven for 40 to 45 minutes or till apples are tender. Let stand a few minutes, and spoon liquid back into apples before serving.

Makes 4 servings.

Peach Cobbler

Filling:

- 3 15-oz cans sugar-free peaches, drained (reserve 1 cup liquid)
- 3 tablespoons cornstarch
- 2 teaspoons stevia blend *or*
  - $^1/_4$ tsp. stevioside
- $^1/_2$ teaspoon cinnamon

Topping:

- 1 cup all-purpose flour
- 1 teaspoon stevia blend *or*
  - $^1/_8$ tsp. stevioside
- 1 teaspoon baking powder
- $^1/_2$ teaspoon cinnamon
- 3 tablespoons butter
- 1 each egg
- 3 tablespoons buttermilk

Filling:

In a heavy saucepan, combine stevia and 3 tablespoons cornstarch. Add 1 cup of reserved liquid. Stir till cornstarch is dissolved. Add 3 drained cans of peaches. Cook and stir till thick.

Topping:

In a medium bowl, mix flour, stevia, baking powder, baking soda, and cinnamon. Cut in butter till mixture resembles coarse crumbs. In a small bowl, combine egg and milk. Add to flour mixture stirring till just moistened. Transfer hot filling to an 8 x 8 x 2-inch baking dish. Drop topping into 6 mounds atop filling. Bake in a 400°F oven 20–25 minutes or till a toothpick inserted into topping comes out clean. Serve warm.

Poached Pears

2 teaspoons stevia blend *or*
  $^1/_4$ tsp. stevioside
1 cup orange juice

1 teaspoon cinnamon
1 teaspoon vanilla
4 each pears, peeled, halved, and
  cored

Bring stevia, orange juice, and vanilla to boiling in a large skillet. Add pears. Reduce heat, cover, and allow to simmer for 10 to 15 minutes or till tender. Serve warm or chilled.

Makes 4 servings.

Fruit Juice Gelatin Blocks

4 envelopes unflavored gelatin
4 teaspoons stevia blend *or*
  $^1/_2$ tsp. stevioside

1 cup cold fruit juice
3 cups fruit juice, heated to
  boiling

In a medium bowl, sprinkle gelatin over cold juice; let stand 2 minutes. Add hot juice and stir until dissolved. Pour into 13 x 9-inch baking pan; chill until set. Cut into 1-inch squares.

Makes about 9 dozen.

Fruity Gelatin

**A GUILT-FREE TREAT WITH AS LITTLE AS
6 CALORIES PER SERVING.**

2 envelopes unflavored gelatin   4 cups Stevia Punch, see index

In a saucepan, sprinkle gelatin over Stevia Punch. Allow to stand 3 minutes. Stirring constantly, heat mixture to a low boil over medium heat. Remove from heat; cool. Pour into desert cups. Chill till set. Makes 8 servings.

Fresh Fruit Yogurt

FAST, EASY, AND SUGAR-FREE.

$\frac{1}{2}$ cup strawberries, sliced (or
    your favorite fruit)
1 cup yogurt
1 $\frac{1}{2}$ teaspoons stevia blend *or*
    $\frac{3}{16}$ tsp. stevioside

$\frac{1}{4}$ teaspoon strawberry flavoring,
    optional

Combine all ingredients in bowl; mix well. Serve chilled. Makes 2 (6-ounce) servings.

Note: Any fruit can be used but, depending on the fruit, you may need to adjust the amount of stevia blend to personal taste.

Yogurt with Fruit Preserves

**THIS FAST, FRUIT YOGURT TASTES BETTER
THAN COMMERCIAL BRANDS.**

1 cup plain yogurt
2 tablespoons sugar-free fruit
   preserves

$1/2$ teaspoon stevia blend *or* $1/16$
   tsp. stevioside

In a small bowl, combine all ingredients. Mix well. Serve chilled.

Makes 1 serving.

Vanilla Ice Cream

5 teaspoons stevia blend *or*
   $5/8$ tsp. stevioside
1 cup milk
1 pinch salt

1 cup half-and-half
2 cups whipping cream
1 $1/2$ teaspoons vanilla extract

Scald milk, stirring constantly. Slowly add stevia until dissolved.
Remove from heat and stir in salt, half-and-half, cream, and vanilla.
Cover and refrigerate until cool. Freeze according to ice-cream maker
manufacturer's instructions.

Makes 8 servings.

Vanilla Ice Milk

REQUIRES NO COOKING.

1 can (13-ounces) evaporated
   milk
7 1/2 teaspoons stevia blend *or*
   7/8 tsp. stevioside

1 1/2 cups whole milk
1 tablespoon vanilla
3 each eggs

Combine evaporated milk and stevia. Beat well until stevia is dissolved. Add whole milk and vanilla extract; beat well. Beat eggs into milk mixture vigorously. Pour into ice-cream maker. Freeze according to ice-cream maker manufacturer's directions.

Makes 6 servings.

Chocolate Ice Cream

4 tablespoons stevia blend *or*
  ¹/₂ tsp. stevioside
3 tablespoons cocoa powder
1 tablespoon cornstarch
¹/₄ teaspoon salt

3 cups milk
2 each eggs, beaten
²/₃ cup half-and-half
1 cup whipping cream
1 teaspoon vanilla extract

Combine stevia, cocoa, cornstarch, and salt in a saucepan. Gradually stir in milk, and cook over medium heat, stirring constantly, until mixture begins to simmer. Gradually stir 1 cup of the hot mixture into the beaten eggs. Stirring constantly, gradually pour egg mixture into remaining hot milk mixture. Continue cooking and stirring over low heat until slightly thickened. Stir in half-and-half, whipping cream, and vanilla. Cover and refrigerate until cold. Freeze according to directions of ice-cream machine manufacturer.

Variation:

Chocolate Chocolate-Chip Ice Cream: For a bittersweet chocolate delight, take 1–2 ounces of Bakers unsweetened chocolate squares and melt them in a double boiler. Add stevia to the melted chocolate until desired sweetness is obtained. Allow to cool but not harden. Spread chocolate on wax paper; allow to harden. Remove paper; break chocolate into small pieces. Halfway through the processing of the ice cream, open the container and slowly stir in the chocolate. Close cover and resume processing of ice cream.

Cappuccino Ice Cream

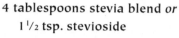

4 tablespoons stevia blend *or*
  1 1/2 tsp. stevioside
1 tablespoon instant coffee
  crystals
2 tablespoons cocoa powder
1 tablespoon cornstarch

1/4 teaspoon salt
3 cups milk
2 each eggs, beaten
2/3 cup half-and-half
1 cup whipping cream
1 teaspoon vanilla extract

In a small bowl, gently beat eggs; set aside. In a saucepan, combine stevia, instant coffee crystals, cocoa, cornstarch, and salt. Gradually stir in milk. Stirring constantly, cook over medium heat until mixture begins to simmer. Gradually stir 1 cup of the hot milk mixture into the beaten eggs. Gradually stir all of the egg mixture into the remaining hot milk mixture in the saucepan. Continue cooking and stirring over low heat until slightly thickened; then cook 2 more minutes. Stir in half-and-half, whipping cream, and vanilla. Cover and refrigerate until cold. Freeze according to directions of ice-cream machine manufacturer.

Makes 8 servings.

Almond Velvet Ice Cream

**THIS NUTTY TREAT REQUIRES NO COOKING
AND NO ICE-CREAM MACHINE.**

2 cups whipping cream
1 cup condensed milk
2 teaspoons stevia blend *or*
  $^1/_4$ tsp. stevioside

1 teaspoon almond flavoring
$^1/_3$ cup almonds, coarsely chopped

Combine cream, condensed milk, stevia, and almond flavoring. Beat
with an electric mixer till soft peaks form. Fold in chopped nuts.
Transfer to an 8 x 8 x 2-inch pan; place in your freezer till firm. Makes
1 quart.

Makes 8 servings.

Orange Frozen Yogurt

1 envelope unflavored gelatin
$^1/_2$ cup cold water
1 6-ounce can frozen orange juice
  concentrate, thawed

3 16-ounce cartons plain, low-fat
  yogurt, unsweetened
$4^1/_2$ tablespoons stevia blend *or*
  $1^1/_2$ tsp. stevioside

In a small, heavy saucepan, combine gelatin and water. Let stand 5
minutes. Stirring constantly, heat until gelatin dissolves. Remove from
heat. In a large mixing bowl, combine thawed orange juice concentrate, yogurt, stevia, and vanilla. Mix in gelatin mixture. Pour into a 4-
quart ice-cream freezer; freeze according to ice-cream maker
manufacturer's directions.

Makes about 8 servings.

Desserts & Candies

Pina Colada Frozen Yogurt

THIS FROZEN TREAT REQUIRES NO COOKING.

$^1/_2$ teaspoon vanilla extract
4 teaspoons stevia blend or
$^1/_2$ tsp. stevioside
$^3/_4$ teaspoon rum extract
4 cups plain yogurt, unsweetened

14 ounces crushed pineapple in
juice
14 ounces coconut milk
$^1/_2$ cup whipping cream

Dissolve stevia into yogurt. Add remaining ingredients; mix well. Freeze according to ice-cream maker manufacturers instructions.

Makes 8 servings.

Creamy Frozen Pops

1 can evaporated milk, chilled
4 teaspoons stevia blend *or*
$^1/_2$ tsp. stevioside

1 teaspoon vanilla
1 package gelatin
$^1/_4$ cup water

In a small saucepan, sprinkle gelatin over $^1/_4$ cup cold water; let stand 5 minutes. Stir over low heat until gelatin is completely dissolved. Allow to cool to room temperature.

In a large bowl, combine cold evaporated milk, stevia, vanilla, and gelatin. With electric mixer, beat till soft peaks form. Spoon mixture into 3-ounce paper cups. Cover with foil. Insert wooden sticks through the foil into the mixture. Freeze till firm.

Dessert Crepes

1 1/2 cups milk
1 cup all-purpose flour
2 each eggs
1 tablespoon cooking oil

2 teaspoons stevia blend *or*
1/4 tsp. stevioside
1/4 teaspoon salt

In a medium mixing bowl, combine flour and stevia; mix well. Add milk, eggs, oil, and salt. Beat till mixed well. Lightly grease a 6-inch skillet; heat. Remove from heat. Spoon 2 tablespoons of the batter into hot pan. Lift and tilt the skillet to spread batter into a thin circle. Return to heat. Brown on one side only. Remove crepe; place on paper towels. Repeat with remaining batter; greasing skillet as needed.

Makes 18 crepes.

Cream Puffs

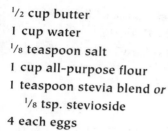

¹/₂ cup butter
1 cup water
¹/₈ teaspoon salt
1 cup all-purpose flour
1 teaspoon stevia blend *or*
   ¹/₈ tsp. stevioside
4 each eggs

Powdered Sugar Replacement,
   optional (see index)

Filling:

pudding, whipped cream, ice
   cream, or fresh fruit

In a small bowl, combine flour and stevia, mix well, and set aside. In a heavy saucepan, combine butter, 1 cup water, and salt. Bring to a boil. While stirring vigorously, add flour mixture to boiling water all at once. Cook, stirring constantly, till mixture forms a ball. Remove from heat; cool slightly. Beating with a wooden spoon, add eggs one at a time. Beat till dough is smooth.

On a greased baking sheet, drop heaping tablespoons of batter 3 inches apart. Bake in a 400°F oven for 30 to 35 minutes or till golden. Cool. Cut puffs in half, and remove any excess dough from inside. Fill with your favorite filling. Sift Powdered Sugar Replacement over tops, if desired.

Makes 10.

Peanut Butter Balls

8 tablespoons cornstarch

8 tablespoons sugar-free peanut butter

4 teaspoons stevia blend *or* 1/2 tsp. stevioside

2 tablespoons Chocolate Chips (see index)

Dipping Chocolate (see index) or Powdered Sugar Replacement (see index)

In a bowl, combine corn starch and stevia. Mix till well blended. Add peanut butter. Knead till well blended and firm. Knead in Chocolate Chips. Form into 16 round balls (about 1 tablespoon each). Dip in Dipping Chocolate, or coat with Powdered Sugar Replacement. Serve immediately or store in refrigerator.

Makes 16 servings.

Fudge Balls

¹/₃ cup butter
3 tablespoons cream
1 teaspoon vanilla extract
¹/₄ cup Dutch cocoa powder

1 cup Powdered Sugar
    Replacement (see index)
Dipping Chocolate (see index) *or*
    flaked coconut

In a bowl, beat butter, cream, and vanilla till creamy. Mix in cocoa powder and Powdered Sugar Replacement. Knead until dough is smooth. Form into small balls. Dip balls in Dipping Chocolate, cool completely, dip again, and cool.

Variation:

Prepare as above, but instead of dipping, roll in flaked coconut, or chopped nuts.

Makes 40 balls.

Chocolate Fudge Treats

1 ounce unsweetened chocolate,
  cut up
8 teaspoons stevia blend *or*
  1 tsp. stevioside

1 teaspoon vanilla
1 cup instant powdered milk
$\frac{1}{3}$ cup cream
$\frac{1}{4}$ cup butter

Over a double boiler, melt unsweetened chocolate and butter at medium heat stirring constantly. Do not let water boil. Still stirring constantly, add 8 teaspoons stevia blend and cream, continuing to cook till heated thoroughly. Remove from heat. Using an electric mixer on medium-low, slowly add the powdered milk. Continue adding powdered milk till a soft dough forms. Shape dough into small bite-sized squares. Serve immediately or cool in the refrigerator. Makes about 1 dozen.

Chocolate Chips

1 cup nonfat dry milk powder
2 ounces unsweetened bakers
   chocolate, chopped
3 tablespoons paraffin wax

$^1/_2$ cup milk
1 tablespoon stevia blend *or*
   $^3/_8$ tsp. stevioside

In a food processor or blender, combine powdered milk, stevia, chopped chocolate, and paraffin; blend to a powder. In a double boiler, combine milk and chocolate mixture. Stirring constantly, cook until chocolate and paraffin are melted. Mixture should be thick and smooth. Remove from heat. Allow to cool slightly. Spread chocolate mixture on wax paper. Allow chocolate to set overnight. Remove chocolate from wax paper, and break into small pieces. If chocolate does not remove easily, warm the back of the waxed paper with your hands. Store in the refrigerator.

Variation:

Dipping Chocolate: Follow directions above, but when mixture is done, do not cool. Keep chocolate slightly warm. Dip candies using a dipping spoon. Shake off excess chocolate. Place on waxed paper and allow to cool completely. Store in the refrigerator.

Powdered Sugar Replacement

2 cups powdered milk

2 cups cornstarch

16 tablespoons stevia blend *or*

8 tsp. stevioside

In a food processor or blender, mix all ingredients to a fine powder. Store in airtight container.

Makes about 5 cups.

CHAPTER 13

Tempting Toppings, Dessert Sauces & Fruit Preserves

TEMPTING TOPPINGS, DESSERT SAUCES & FRUIT PRESERVES

Apple Butter – 206

Apricot Rum Sauce – 196

Banana Sauce – 197

Bittersweet Chocolate Glaze – 192

Blueberry Syrup – 200

Butterscotch Sauce – 195

Chantilly Cream Frosting – 191

Cherry Sauce – 198

Chocolate Cream Cheese Frosting – 193

Chocolate Sauce – 193

Chocolate Whipped Cream – 205

Cinnamon Stevia – 203

Freezer Jam – 208

Fruit Juice Jelly – 209

Hot Fudge Sauce – 194

Lite Whipped Topping – 204

Low-Fat Strawberry Cream Cheese Spread – 202

Maple Flavored Syrup – 201

Mocha Sauce – 194

Orange or Lemon Cream Cheese Glaze – 192

Orange Sauce – 199

Peach Butter – 207

Stevia Butter – 203

Stirred Custard Sauce – 199

Vanilla Cream Cheese Frosting – 191

Whipped Cream – 205

Vanilla Cream Cheese Frosting

EXCELLENT FOR CAKES, MUFFINS, AND COOKIES.

2 8-oz. packages cream cheese
4 teaspoons stevia blend *or* ¹/₂ tsp. stevioside
1 teaspoon vanilla

In a mixing bowl, beat cream cheese at medium speed till fluffy. Sprinkle stevia blend over cream cheese. Beat well, using a rubber spatula to scrape the sides of the bowl often. Add vanilla; beat till combined. Frosts 1 cake. Refrigerate unused portions up to 5 days.

Makes about 2 cups.

Chantilly Cream Frosting

4 tablespoons cornstarch
1 cup skim milk
4 teaspoons stevia blend *or*
   ¹/₂ tsp. stevioside

5 tablespoons powdered milk
2 teaspoons vanilla
³/₄ cup butter

Mix cornstarch, skim milk, stevia, and powdered milk in a saucepan. Cook until thickened, stirring constantly. Remove from heat, and add vanilla. Allow to cool completely. In a bowl, whip butter till creamy. Add the cooled mixture to butter and beat well. Refrigerate until ready to use.

Makes about 2 cups – enough to ice a two layer cake.

Orange or Lemon Cream Cheese Glaze

1 8-oz. package reduced-fat
  cream cheese, softened
1 teaspoon orange or lemon extract

1 ½ teaspoons stevia blend *or*
  ³/₁₆ tsp. stevioside
skim milk

Mix cream cheese, extract, stevia blend, and enough milk to make medium glaze consistency.

Makes about 1 cup.

Perfect over angle food cake or lemon cake. Makes a nice glaze for cookies.

Bittersweet Chocolate Glaze

**TRY DRIZZLING OVER CAKE OR ICE CREAM.
MAKES A GREAT FONDUE.**

3 ounces unsweetened baking
  chocolate, cut into small pieces
¼ cup skim milk

1 tablespoon butter
5 teaspoons stevia blend *or*
  ⁵/₈ tsp. stevioside

Combine chocolate, stevia blend, and milk in small saucepan or double boiler. Cook over low heat, stirring frequently, just until chocolate begins to melt. Remove from heat. Stir until mixture is smooth. Allow to cool until glaze is thick enough to spread. *Makes about ½ cup.*

Chocolate Cream Cheese Frosting

THIS DECADENT TOPPING IS OUR FAMILY'S FAVORITE.

2 8-oz. packages fat-free cream
  cheese, at room temperature
7 teaspoons stevia blend *or*
  $^7/_8$ tsp. stevioside

3 tablespoons skim milk
$^1/_3$ cup Dutch-process cocoa
1 teaspoon vanilla

In a medium mixing bowl, beat cream cheese, stevia, and 1 tablespoon milk until fluffy. Beat in cocoa, vanilla, and enough remaining milk to bring frosting to a spreadable consistency.

Makes about 2 cups.

Chocolate Sauce

**SERVE HOT OVER ICE CREAM, CAKE,
WAFFLES, OR PANCAKES.**

2 squares unsweetened baking
  chocolate
6 teaspoons stevia blend *or*
  $^3/_4$ tsp. stevioside

$^3/_4$ cup skim milk
1 teaspoon vanilla

In a heavy pan or double boiler, dissolve 2 tablespoons stevia blend with $^3/_4$ cup of skim milk. Add the baking chocolate; heat, stirring, until chocolate is melted. Remove from heat and stir in vanilla.

Makes about 1 cup.

Hot Fudge Sauce

A SUGAR-FREE VERSION OF THE REAL THING.

1 ounce unsweetened chocolate, cut up
8 teaspoons stevia blend *or* 1 tsp. stevioside

1 teaspoon vanilla
$^1/_2$ cup powdered milk
$^1/_2$ cup whipping cream.
$^1/_4$ cup butter

Over a double boiler, melt unsweetened chocolate and butter at medium heat, stirring frequently. Do not let water boil. Stir in 8 teaspoons stevia blend and cream; allow to simmer, stirring occasionally, until heated thoroughly. Remove from heat. Using an electric mixer on medium-low, slowly add powdered milk. Serve over ice cream or cake. Refrigerate any unused portion for up to 5 days.

Mocha Sauce

1 cup skim milk
4 teaspoons unsweetened cocoa
2 teaspoons cornstarch
1 teaspoon instant coffee crystals

1 teaspoon vanilla
2 teaspoons stevia blend *or* $^1/_4$ tsp. stevioside

In small, heavy saucepan, combine milk, cocoa, cornstarch, stevia, and coffee crystals. Cook, stirring constantly, until thickened and boiling. Reduce heat; continue cooking and stirring 2 more minutes. Remove from heat, stir in vanilla, and cool. Cover and refrigerate till cold.

Makes about 1 cup.

Tempting Toppings, Dessert Sauces & Fruit Preserves

Butterscotch Sauce

SERVE OVER VANILLA ICE CREAM, CREPES, OR FLAN.

1 cup apple juice
1 tablespoon cornstarch
1 tablespoon margarine

4 teaspoons stevia blend *or*
   ¹/₂ tsp. stevioside
1 teaspoon butterscotch flavoring
1 teaspoon vanilla

Combine apple juice, stevia, and cornstarch in small saucepan. Cook, stirring constantly, over medium heat until thick and bubbly. Continue cooking and stirring 2 more minutes. Remove from heat. Stir in margarine, butterscotch flavoring, and vanilla.

Makes 1 cup.

Apricot Rum Sauce

EXCELLENT FOR WAFFLES, PANCAKES, OR ICE CREAM.

4 each ripe apricots, pealed and
   pitted
2 tablespoons rum flavoring
$1/2$ cup water

1 each lemon juice
$1\,1/2$ teaspoons stevia blend *or*
   $3/16$ tsp. stevioside

Combine apricots, water, stevia, and lemon juice in a heavy sauce pan and heat over medium heat stirring frequently until apricots soften; bring to a boil. Remove from heat and add the rum flavoring; allow to cool. In a blender or food processor, puree sauce till thick and creamy. Refrigerate; serve cold.

Variations:

Plums or peaches can be substituted for the apricots.

Note: The fruit must be very ripe or the sauce will be tart.

Banana Sauce

1 each banana, thinly sliced
¹/₂ each lemon, or 1 tablespoon
    lemon juice
1 tablespoon maraschino liqueur

1 ¹/₂ teaspoons stevia blend *or*
    ³/₁₆ tsp. stevioside
2 teaspoons arrowroot or
    cornstarch

Put the lemon juice, water, and maraschino liqueur into a pan with stevia, and dissolve stevia over low heat, stirring frequently. Make a paste of the arrowroot or cornstarch with a tablespoon of water. Stir paste into the hot liquid and cook, stirring constantly, until the sauce thickens and is clear. Add the sliced banana and serve hot.

Makes a perfect filling for crepes, or a topping for pancakes, waffles, or ice cream.

Cherry Sauce

1 pound cherries, pitted
1 1/2 teaspoons stevia blend *or*
   3/16 tsp. stevioside
1 pinch ground cinnamon

1/2 cup water
1 teaspoon lemon juice
2 teaspoons arrowroot
1 tablespoon water

Combine pitted cherries and lemon juice in a pan with stevia blend. Cover and set on low heat until the juice runs freely. Remove cherries with a slotted spoon leaving the juice in the pan. Set cherries aside. Add 1/2 cup water to the juice; simmer 5 minutes uncovered, stirring occasionally. Taste for sweetness and adjust to your liking. If too sweet, add a little more lemon juice. Make a paste of the arrowroot with 1 tablespoon of water. Stir paste into the cherry syrup. Bring, stirring, just to a boil; remove from heat. The liquid should be the consistency of heavy cream. Add the cherries to the pan; stir till well mixed.

Makes about 3 cups.

Cherry sauce is excellent over cakes, over ice cream, or as a filling for crepes.

Orange Sauce

¾ cup orange juice
1 tablespoon cornstarch

1 ½ teaspoons stevia blend *or*
³⁄₁₆ tsp. stevioside

In a small, heavy saucepan, mix orange juice, stevia, and cornstarch; heat to boiling stirring constantly. Reduce heat. Simmer, stirring constantly, until thickened (about 3 minutes). Remove from heat. Cool to room temperature; refrigerate until chilled.

Makes 6 servings.

Stirred Custard Sauce

3 each eggs, beaten
2 cups light cream

3 teaspoons stevia blend *or*
³⁄₈ tsp. stevioside
1 teaspoon vanilla

In a heavy, medium saucepan, combine eggs, cream, and stevia. Cook, stirring constantly, over medium heat until the custard just coats a metal spoon. Remove from heat and stir in vanilla. Pour custard mixture into a bowl. Cover surface with clear plastic wrap. Chill till serving time. Create your own flavor by adding 3 tablespoons of flavored liqueur instead of the vanilla.

Makes 6-8 servings.

The perfect addition to bread pudding, cake, or to top off fruit. Also makes a delicious fondue for cubes of cake or sliced fruit.

Blueberry Syrup

1 cup blueberries
$^1/_2$ cup apple juice
1 $^1/_2$ teaspoons cornstarch

2 teaspoons stevia blend *or*
   $^1/_4$ tsp. stevioside
1 tablespoon lemon juice
1 tablespoon margarine or butter

Combine berries and apple juice in a blender or food processor; blend till pureed. In a heavy saucepan, combine blueberry puree, stevia, and cornstarch; mix well. Cook, stirring constantly, till thick and bubbly. Continue cooking and stirring for 2 more minutes. Remove from heat. Stir in lemon juice and butter.

Makes 1 cup.

Serve over pancakes, waffles, or French toast.

Maple Flavored Syrup

1 cup apple juice
1 tablespoon cornstarch
1 tablespoon margarine
3 teaspoons stevia blend *or*
   $^{3}/_{8}$ tsp. stevioside

1 teaspoon maple flavoring
1 teaspoon vanilla

Combine apple juice, stevia and cornstarch in small saucepan. Stirring constantly, cook, over medium heat until thick and bubbly. Continue cooking and stirring 2 minutes more. Remove from heat. Stir in margarine, maple flavoring, and vanilla.

Makes 1 cup.

Serve over pancakes, waffles, or French toast.

Low-Fat Strawberry Cream Cheese Spread

GREAT ON TOAST OR BAGELS.

1 8-ounces package low-fat cream cheese, at room temperature
2 teaspoons stevia blend or $1/8$ tsp. stevioside
$1/2$ teaspoon strawberry flavoring

In a mixing bowl, beat cream cheese at medium speed till fluffy. Sprinkle stevia blend over cream cheese. Beat well, scraping sides of bowl often. Add strawberry flavoring. Beat till thoroughly combined. Serve immediately. Refrigerate any unused portions for up to 5 days.

Makes about 1 cup.

Stevia Butter

$^1/_2$ cup butter, room temperature
1 teaspoon stevia blend *or* $^1/_8$ tsp. stevioside

In a small mixing bowl, cream butter till fluffy. Sprinkle stevia blend over the butter. Mix well, scraping the sides of the bowl often. Serve immediately. Refrigerate any unused portions.

Makes about 1/2 cup.

Cinnamon Stevia

$^1/_2$ cup powdered milk
1 tablespoon cinnamon

2 teaspoons stevia blend *or*
$^1/_4$ tsp. stevioside

Combine all ingredients in a blender or food processor. Process until it has the consistency of flour. Sift over cake, cookies, pancakes, waffles, or French toast.

Lite Whipped Topping

1 can condensed milk
1/3 cup water
1 package gelatin

2 teaspoons stevia blend *or*
1/4 tsp. stevioside
1 teaspoon vanilla

Refrigerate can of condensed milk till well chilled, at least 4 hours. In a small saucepan, mix cold water and gelatin; allow to sit for five minutes. Over medium heat, cook gelatin mixture till bubbly. Allow to cool to room temperature. Make an ice bath: take a large bowl and fill with ice, placing a smaller bowl on top of the ice. Pour the condensed milk, gelatin mixture, stevia, and vanilla in smaller bowl.

On high speed of an electric mixer, beat milk mixture till soft peaks form. Best when served immediately. Refrigerate any unused portions for up to 5 days.

Makes about 4 cups.

Whipped Cream

1 cup whipping cream
1 teaspoon stevia blend *or* ⅛ tsp. stevioside
1 teaspoon vanilla

In a bowl combine whipping cream, stevia blend, and vanilla. Beat on medium speed till soft peaks form.

Makes 2 cups.

If you overbeat cream, it will turn to butter. But don't worry – just poor off the buttermilk and enjoy a sweet spread on your toast or muffin.

Variation:

Chocolate Whipped Cream: Prepare as above, sifting in 2 tablespoons unsweetened cocoa powder plus 1 teaspoon additional stevia blend.

Apple Butter

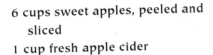

6 cups sweet apples, peeled and
  sliced

1 cup fresh apple cider

3 teaspoons stevia blend *or*
  3/8 tsp. stevioside

1 tablespoon ground cinnamon
  (optional)

In a heavy saucepan, place apples and cider over medium heat.
Stirring frequently, cook until mixture comes to a boil. Lower heat and
simmer, still stirring frequently, for about 60 minutes, or till apples
have disintegrated and mixture is thick. Remove from heat. Stir in
stevia and cinnamon, if desired. Pour into jars and refrigerate for up to
2 weeks.

Makes 4 cups.

Use as a spread or as a dessert topping.

Peach Butter

3 pounds peaches, peeled, pitted
   and sliced
3/4 cup white grape juice
1–2 teaspoons ground cinnamon

$^1/_2$ teaspoon ground nutmeg
$^1/_8$ teaspoon ground cloves
8 teaspoons stevia blend *or*
   I tsp. stevioside

In a large, heavy saucepan, combine peaches, juice, spices, and stevia. Stirring occasionally, bring to boiling. Cover and simmer until fruit can be easily mashed with a fork (about 15 minutes). Cool slightly. Puree in blender or food processor. Return to saucepan. Simmer, uncovered, over low heat until desired consistency, stirring frequently. (This may take up to 1 hour.) Remove from heat. Transfer to freezer containers or jars, leaving a $^1/_2$-inch head space. Place in the refrigerator until cool (about 3 hours). Transfer to the freezer. Store up to 2 weeks in refrigerator or up to 3 months in freezer.

Makes 6 cups.

Freezer Jam

3 cups crushed fruit, room temperature
1 package fruit pectin for sugar-free jams and jellies
5–7 teaspoons stevia blend (depending on sweetness of fruit) *or*
   $^5/_8$–1 tsp. stevioside
1 cup water

In a bowl, combine the crushed fruit with stevia; set aside. Pour 1 cup of water in a heavy saucepan. Stir the pectin into the water slowly to prevent lumping. Stirring constantly, bring pectin-water mixture to a boil. Boil 2 minutes more, still stirring constantly. Pour the hot pectin-water mixture into crushed fruit. Stir thoroughly, about 4 minutes. Pour into freezer containers, leaving a $^1/_2$-inch head space; cover with tight-fitting lids, and refrigerate. After jam has set (about 3 hours), transfer to freezer. Makes an excellent cake filling, or ice-cream topping.

Fruit Juice Jelly

FAST AND EASY; FOR THE FREEZER OR THE REFRIGERATOR.

1 pkg. fruit pectin for sugar-free jams and jellies
4 cups your favorite juice
7–10 teaspoons stevia blend *or* $^7/_8$–1$^1/_4$ tsp. stevioside

In a heavy saucepan, combine juice and one package of lite fruit pectin. Let mixture set 5–10 minutes, then bring to a full boil over high heat, stirring constantly. Boil for 2 minutes longer, still stirring constantly. Remove from heat and add stevia to taste. Stir well. Pour into clean freezer containers, leaving a $^1/_2$-inch head space; cover with tight-fitting lid, and refrigerate. After jam has set (about 3 hours), transfer to freezer.

Makes 4 cups.

CHAPTER 14

Condiments, Sauces & Relishes

CONDIMENTS, SAUCES & RELISHES

Old Fashioned Catsup

2 cups tomato sauce
$^{1}/_{4}$ cup apple cider vinegar
1 teaspoon stevia blend *or*
   $^{1}/_{8}$ tsp. stevioside

$^{1}/_{4}$ teaspoon onion powder
1 tablespoon cornstarch or
   arrowroot
1 teaspoon water

In a small cup, mix water and cornstarch or arrowroot. Stir until dissolved. In a large saucepan, combine all ingredients; mix well. Stirring constantly, bring to a gentle boil. Still stirring constantly, reduce heat and simmer to desired thickness. Refrigerate until needed.

Makes about 1 $^{1}/_{2}$ cups.

Tangy Catsup

1 cup apple cider vinegar	¹/₂ teaspoon red pepper
1 teaspoon ground cinnamon	1 tablespoon salt
1 teaspoon celery seed	5 teaspoons stevia blend *or*
2 24-ounce cans tomatoes, diced	⁵/₈ tsp. stevioside
¹/₂ cup onions, minced	2 tablespoons tomato paste

In a small saucepan, stir together vinegar, cinnamon, and celery seed; bring to a boil. Set aside. In a heavy stock pot or large saucepan, mix together remaining ingredients; bring to a boil stirring occasionally. Reduce heat. Add vinegar mix. Simmer for 30 minutes stirring occasionally. In small batches, puree in blender or food processor. Return to pot; simmer, stirring occasionally, until thick.

Makes about 4 cups.

You can speed up the thickening process by adding a paste of 2 tablespoons of cornstarch or arrowroot mixed with ¹/₄ cup cold water.

Variation:

Spicy Catsup: Add 3 teaspoons of hot sauce during the simmering stage.

Condiments, Sauces & Relishes

Mexicali Barbecue Sauce

¹/₂ cup Picante Sauce (see index)
1 tablespoon tomato paste

2 teaspoons stevia blend *or*
¹/₄ tsp. stevioside
1 tablespoon Dijon mustard

In a bowl, dissolve stevia into picante sauce. Mix remaining ingredients into picante sauce. Stir until well mixed. Keep refrigerated until needed. Use as a baste or sauce.

Makes about 1 cup.

Mustard Barbecue Sauce

1 cup prepared yellow mustard
²/₃ cup apple cider vinegar
1 tablespoon Worcestershire
sauce
1 ¹/₂ cups catsup (see index)

¹/₂ teaspoon maple flavoring
2 tablespoons olive oil
¹/₂ teaspoon black pepper
9 teaspoons stevia blend *or*
1 tsp. stevioside

Combine all ingredients in a medium sauce pan. Simmer over medium heat, stirring occasionally, until sauce is well blended and hot. Remove from heat; allow to cool. Keep refrigerated until needed. Use as a baste or sauce.

Makes about 2 cups.

Cocktail Sauce

1 cup Old Fashioned Catsup (see
  index)
3 tablespoons grated onion
3 tablespoons prepared horse
  radish

2 tablespoons lemon juice
2 tablespoons minced fresh
  tarragon
Tabasco to taste

Wisk all ingredients in a medium bowl to blend. Cover and refrigerate at least 1 hour. For a bit more spice try using Tangy Catsup (see index).

Makes 1 1/2 cups.

Condiments, Sauces & Relishes

Picante Sauce

1 24-ounce can tomatoes, finely
  diced, reserve juice
6 ounces reserved tomato juice
1 small onion, finely chopped
1 4-ounce can green chili peppers,
  finely chopped
2 tablespoons fresh cilantro,
  minced

1 tablespoon lime juice
2 teaspoons stevia blend *or*
  $^1/_4$ tsp. stevioside
1 teaspoon salt
1 teaspoon pepper
1 each jalapeno, finely chopped

In a bowl, combine all ingredients; mix well. Refrigerate at least 2 hours.

Makes about 4 cups.

Note: If you like it HOT, add an extra jalapeno or two, or, for the really brave, add a finely chopped Habanero pepper.

Black Bean Salsa

3 medium tomatoes, finely diced
1 15-ounces can black beans, drained
1 4-ounce can green chili peppers, drained, finely chopped
3 tablespoons cilantro, fresh, chopped
1 small onion, finely chopped

1 clove garlic, minced
1 each jalapeno, finely chopped
1 teaspoon stevia blend *or* $^{1}/_{8}$ tsp. stevioside
3 tablespoons lime juice
$^{1}/_{4}$ teaspoon cinnamon
salt and pepper to taste

In a small bowl, dissolve stevia into the lime juice. Set aside. In another bowl combine all of the other ingredients. Add lime mixture; mix well. Refrigerate at least 2 hours before serving.

Makes about 4$^{1}/_{2}$ cups.

Note: If you like it HOT, add an extra jalapeno or two, or, for the really brave, add a finely chopped Habanero pepper.

Corn Relish

2 15-ounce cans corn, drained
1/2 cup celery, chopped
3/4 cup sweet red bell pepper,
   diced
3/4 cup green bell pepper, diced
1 medium onion, chopped
1 1/4 cups apple cider vinegar

9 teaspoons stevia blend *or*
   1 tsp. stevioside
1 tablespoon salt
1 teaspoon celery seed
1/4 cup flour
1 tablespoon dry mustard
1/2 teaspoon ground turmeric

In a kettle, combine corn, celery, red and green peppers, onion, 3/4 cup vinegar, stevia, salt, and celery seed. Bring to a boil stirring occasionally. In a small bowl combine 1/2 cup vinegar, flour, dry mustard, and turmeric. Add to corn mixture. Stirring constantly, bring to a boil. Continue cooking and stirring 1 minute more. Ladle into pint jars. Refrigerate.

Makes 3 pints.

Refrigerator Sweet Pickles

FAST AND EASY

4 cups cucumbers, thinly sliced
2 cloves garlic, halved
1³/₄ cups water
1 teaspoon mustard seed
1 teaspoon celery seed
1 teaspoon ground turmeric

2 cups onions, sliced
1 cup carrots, julienne-strip
2 cups apple cider vinegar
9 teaspoons stevia blend *or*
   1 tsp. stevioside

Place sliced cucumbers and garlic in a glass bowl. (Do not use metal.) Set aside. In a saucepan, stir together turmeric, mustard seed, celery seed, stevia, and water. Bring to boiling. Stir in onions and carrots. Boil for 2 minutes. Stir in vinegar; cook 1 minute more. Pour over cucumbers and garlic. Cool. Cover and refrigerate at least 24 hours before serving.

Makes about 5 cups.

Condiments, Sauces & Relishes

Cranberry Sauce

1 12-ounce package fresh cranberries
9 teaspoons stevia blend *or* 1 tsp. stevioside
1 cup white grape juice

In a saucepan, combine stevia and juice. Bring to a rapid boil. Add cranberries. Stirring constantly, boil gently over medium-high heat for 6–7 minutes or until cranberry skins pop. Remove from heat. Serve warm or chilled.

Makes about 3 cups.

Orange-Cranberry Sauce

1 12-ounce package fresh cranberries
10 teaspoons stevia blend *or* 1 1/4 tsp. stevioside
1 cup orange juice
1 teaspoon orange flavoring

In a saucepan, combine stevia and juice. Bring to a rapid boil stirring constantly. Add cranberries. Still stirring constantly, boil gently over medium-high heat for 6–7 minutes or until cranberry skins pop. Remove from heat and stir in orange flavoring. Serve warm or chilled.

Makes about 3 cups.

Sweet & Sour Sauce

³/₄ cup water
¹/₃ cup catsup (see index)
¹/₃ cup apple cider or white wine
    vinegar

1 tablespoon soy sauce
2 tablespoons cornstarch or
    arrowroot
5 teaspoons stevia blend *or*
    ⁵/₈ tsp. stevioside

In a heavy saucepan, combine water, vinegar, ketchup, stevia and soy sauce. Stir in cornstarch. Over medium heat, cook, stirring constantly, until thick and bubbly, then continue cooking and stirring for 1 minute more. Remove from heat. Serve over vegetables, meat or meat substitute.

Makes about 1 cup.

White Sauce

1 tablespoon butter
1 tablespoon all-purpose flour

¹/₂ teaspoon stevia blend *or*
    ¹/₁₆ tsp. stevioside
³/₄ cup milk

In a saucepan, melt butter. Stir in flour, salt, stevia and pepper. Stirring constantly, cook till golden (about 2 minutes). Slowly stir in milk. Over medium heat, continue cooking and stirring until thick. Serve immediately.

Makes about ³/₄ cup.

Condiments, Sauces & Relishes

Appendix

Suppliers of Stevia Extracts and Plants

The following list is for informational purposes only to help you, the consumer, find stevia. They are listed in alphabetical order. None of these companies have paid any compensation to be listed here.

Suppliers of Stevia Extracts

Body Ecology, Inc.
< www.geocities.com/
HotSprings/Spa/3375/ >
800-478-3842

The Cornucopia
www.thecornucopia.com
1104 Thorpe Lane
San Marcos, Texas 78666
888-353-5044

The Herbal Advantage
www.herbaladvantage.com
Route 3 Box 93
Rogersville, MO 65742-9214
800-753-9199

Mother Nature
www.mothernature.com
965 Street Rd.
Southhampton, PA 18966
800-517-9020

Now Foods
www.nowvitamins.com
550 Mitchell
Glendale Heights, IL 60139
800-999-8069

NuNaturals
www.nunaturals.com
2220 W. 2nd Ave. #1
Eugene, OR 97402
800-753-4372

Rainforest Bio-Energetics
www.galaxymall.com/com-
merce/rainforest/products.html
1002 Jupiter Park Lane
Jupiter, FL 33456
800-835-0850

Stevita Co., Inc.
www.stevitastevia.com
7650 US Hwy. 287, #100
Arlington, Texas 76001
888-STEVITA (783-8482)

Wisdom of the Ancients
www.healthfree.com/stevia.htm
640 S. Perry Lane #2
Tempe, AZ 85287
800-947-6417

Here are two companies that sell stevia plants:

The Herbal Advantage
www.herbaladvantage.com
Route 3 Box 93
Rogersville, MO 65742-9214
800-753-9199

Mountain Valley Growers
www.mountainvalleygrowers.com
38325 Pepperweed Rd.
Squaw Valley, CA 93675
559-338-2775

This list is only a few of the many companies that distribute stevia. For a more complete list, which is updated frequently, see the "Cooking with Stevia" webpage at:
http://www.steviapetition.org

Stevia Conversions

Packets to Packets*

Sugar	Stevia Blends	Aspartame	Saccharin	Acesulfame-k
1 packet	1 packet	1 packet	1 packet	1 packet

Artificial Sweetener Packets to Stevia Extracts*

Artificial Sweetener (packets)	Stevia Blends (Spoonable Stevia) Bulk Form (teaspoons)	Clear Stevia Liquid (teaspoons)	Pure Stevioside (teaspoons)
1	$1/2$	about $1/4$	$1/16$
6	3	about $1/2$	$3/8$
8	4	about $3/4$	$1/2$
12	6	$1 1/4$	$3/4$
18	9	$1 3/4$	$1 1/8$
24	12	$2 1/2$	$1 1/2$
48	24	$5 1/4$	3

*The sweetening strength of stevia extracts will vary from brand to brand (see Chapter 2, Types of Stevia). When heated, stevia does not lose its sweet taste the way aspartame does. Therefore, when replacing aspartame with stevia, some adjustments may be needed.

Sugar to Stevia Extracts*

Sugar	Stevia Blends (Spoonable Stevia) in Packets	Stevia Blends (Spoonable Stevia) Bulk Form	Clear Stevia Liquid	Pure Stevioside
2 teaspoons	1 packet	½ teaspoon	about ¼ teaspoon	1/16 teaspoon
¼ cup	6 packets	3 teaspoons	about ½ teaspoon	3/8 teaspoon
⅓ cup	8 packets	4 teaspoons	about ¾ teaspoon	½ teaspoon
½ cup	12 packets	6 teaspoons	1¼ teaspoons	¾ teaspoon
¾ cup	18 packets	9 teaspoons	1¾ teaspoons	1 teaspoon
1 cup	24 packets	12 teaspoons	2½ teaspoons	1½ teaspoons
2 cups	48 packets	24 teaspoons	5¼ teaspoons	3 teaspoons

Stevia Petition

YOU WILL MAKE A DIFFERENCE!

Stevia is a natural sweetener used internationally by millions – except in the United States. In the land of the free and the brave this herb is being discriminated against by the Food and Drug Administration (FDA). You can fight the injustice of the FDA by contacting your government representatives today!

Stevia should be approved as a food and not just a dietary supplement photocopy this petition, fill it out and mail it to your Congressional Representative and your two Senate Representatives. With your help, we will win this battle.

This petition is also available on-line at www.steviapetition.org.

NAME
_____

ADDRESS
_____

CITY, STATE, ZIP
_____

COUNTRY
_____

HOME PHONE
_____

E-MAIL ADDRESS
_____

DATE
_____

REPRESENTATIVE'S NAME
_____

ADDRESS
_____

_____

Dear _____ :

I am writing to express my outrage at the Food and Drug
Administration's mishandling of the herb STEVIA in the United States.
While other nations are able to use this wonderful herb as a sugar
substitute, Americans are limited to using it as a "dietary supplement".
Why is this? STEVIA is approved for use as a food and food ingredient
in countries around the world—because it is all-natural, non-toxic,
non-caloric, helpful to the environment, a valuable cash crop, and safe
for diabetics, hence completely safe for human use—but FDA restricts
its use by Americans. Effectively banned within the United States,
STEVIA plants are not even grown by American farmers.

With the passage of the 1994 Dietary Supplement Health and Education Act (DSHEA), Congress rightly gave the power back to the people
concerning whether or not to improve their health with the use of
natural products previously kept out of reach. DSHEA also permitted
Americans to use STEVIA but only as a dietary supplement. Despite
this legal protection, the FDA has done everything within its power to
try to prevent the importation and distribution of STEVIA in the United
States. Petitions to have STEVIA receive GRAS (Generally Accepted as
Safe) status were denied by the FDA. FDA employs delay tactics, such
as requesting unreasonable amounts of statistical data about this
plant's agricultural and commercial history prior to 1958.

In 1997, the CBS news magazine 60 Minutes aired a report revealing a
conflict of interest between FDA and one manufacturer of artificial
sweeteners. This manufacturer had "influenced" the director of the
FDA to get the approval of aspartame as a food additive during the
1980s when there were many questionable reports on its safety. Today
the FDA receives more complaints about aspartame than about any
other product. It is believed that the cozy relationship between FDA
and the artificial sweetener industry is why STEVIA has largely been
kept out of reach of the American consumer.

Is STEVIA safe? Absolutely. Research proves this—research the FDA ignores. Moreover, STEVIA has been used extensively around the world as an ingredient in foods WITHOUT A SINGLE CASE OF UNDESIRABLE EFFECTS. This fact alone should qualify as proof that the product is safe for use as an all-natural sweetener.

Do the American people want STEVIA? Count on it. Americans are more and more averse to the use of artificial substances in their diets. The herb STEVIA is especially beneficial for people who suffer from diabetes, hypoglycemia, candida, and other ailments where regular use of sugar and artificial sweeteners is ill-advised.

As my elected representative, you ought to review the entire controversy surrounding the herb STEVIA. FDA's unconscionable withholding of this natural substance from the American people must be answered, once and for all.

Make good on DSHEA. Give STEVIA full legal status.

Yours truly,

Helpful Tips

Measurements

a pinch . . . . ⅛ teaspoon or less

3 teaspoons . . . . 1 tablespoon

4 tablespoons . . . . ¼ cup

8 tablespoons . . . . ½ cup

12 tablespoons . . . . ¾ cup

16 tablespoons . . . . 1 cup

2 cups . . . . 1 pint

4 cups . . . . 1 quart

4 quarts . . . . 1 gallon

8 quarts . . . . 1 peck

16 ounces . . . . 1 pound

32 ounces . . . . 1 quart

8 ounces liquid . . . . 1 cup

1 ounce liquid . . . . 2 tablespoons

(For liquid and dry measurements use standard measuring spoons and cups. All measurements are level.)

Substitutions

Ingredient	Quantity	Substitute
self rising flour	1 cup	1 cup all-purpose flour, ¹/₂ tsp. salt, and 1 tsp. baking powder
cornstarch	1 tbsp.	2 tbsp. flour or 2 tsp. quick-cooking tapioca
baking powder	1 tsp.	¹/₂ tsp. baking soda plus ¹/₂ tsp. cream of tartar
powdered sugar	1 cup	1 cup granulated sugar plus 1 tsp. cornstarch
brown sugar	¹/₂ cup	2 tbsp. molasses in ¹/₂ cup granulated sugar
sour milk	1 cup	1 tbsp. lemon juice or vinegar plus sweet milk to make 1 cup (let stand 5 minutes)
whole milk	1 cup	¹/₂ cup evaporated milk plus ¹/₂ cup water
cracker crumbs	¹/₂ cup	1 cup bread crumbs
chocolate	1 oz.	3 or 4 tbsp. cocoa plus 1 tbsp. butter*
fresh herbs	1 tbsp.	1 tsp. dried herbs
fresh onion	1 small	1 tbsp. instant minced onion, rehydrated
dry mustard	1 tsp.	1 tbsp. prepared mustard
tomato juice	1 cup	¹/₂ cup tomato sauce plus ¹/₂ cup water
catsup	1 cup	1 cup tomato sauce plus ¹/₂ cup sugar and 2 tbsp. vinegar
dates	1 lb.	1¹/₂ cup dates, pitted and cut
bananas	3 medium	1 cup mashed
mini marshmallows	10	1 large marshmallow

*In substituting cocoa for chocolate in cakes, the amount of flour must be reduced.

Brown and white sugars: usually may be used interchangeably.

Vegetable Time Table

Vegetable	Cooking Method	Time
Asparagus	Boiled	10–15 minutes
Artichokes, French	Boiled	40 minutes
	Steamed	45–60 minutes
Beans, Lima	Boiled	20–40 minutes
	Steamed	60 minutes
Beans, String	Boiled	15–35 minutes
	Steamed	60 minutes
Beets, young with skin	Boiled	30 minutes
	Steamed	60 minutes
	Baked	70–90 minutes
Beets, old	Boiled or Steamed	1–2 hours
Broccoli, flowerets	Boiled	5–10 minutes
Broccoli, stems	Boiled	20–30 minutes
Brussel Sprouts	Boiled	20–30 minutes
Cabbage, chopped	Boiled	10–20 minutes
	Steamed	25 minutes
Cauliflower, stem down	Boiled	20–30 minutes
Cauliflower, flowerets	Boiled	8–10 minutes
Carrots, cut across	Boiled	8–10 minutes
	Steamed	40 minutes
Corn, green, tender	Boiled	5–10 minutes
	Steamed	15 minutes
	Baked	20 minutes
Corn on the cob	Boiled	8–10 minutes
	Steamed	15 minutes
Eggplant, whole	Boiled	30 minutes
	Steamed	40 minutes
	Baked	45 minutes
Parsnips	Boiled	25–40 minutes
	Steamed	60 minutes
	Baked	60–75 minutes
Peas, green	Boiled or Steamed	5–15 minutes
Potatoes	Boiled	20–40 minutes
	Steamed	60 minutes
	Baked	45–60 minutes
Pumpkin or Squash	Boiled	20–40 minutes
	Steamed	45 minutes
	Baked	60 minutes
Tomatoes	Boiled	5–15 minutes
Turnips	Boiled	25–40 minutes

Equivalency Chart

Food	Quantity	Yield
unsifted flour	3½ cups	1 pound
sifted flour	4 cups	1 pound
sifted cake flour	4½ cups	1 pound
rye flour	5 cups	1 pound
flour	1 pound	4 cups
baking powder	5½ ounces	1 cup
cornmeal	3 cups	1 pound
cornstarch	3 cups	1 pound
lemon	1 medium	3 tbsp. juice
apple	1 medium	1 cup
orange	3–4 medium	1 cup juice
onion	1 medium	½ cup
unshelled walnuts	1 pound	1½ cups
sugar	2 cups	1 pound
powdered sugar	3½ cups	1 pound
brown sugar	2½ cups	1 pound
spaghetti	7 ounces	4 cups cooked
noodles (uncooked)	4 ounces	2–3 cups cooked
macaroni (uncooked)	4 ounces	2½ cups cooked
macaroni (cooked)	6 cups	8-ounce package
noodles (cooked)	7 cups	8-ounce package
long-grain rice (uncooked)	1 cup	3–4 cups cooked
saltine crackers	28 crackers	1 cup fine crumbs
butter	1 stick	½ cup
cocoa	4 cups	1 pound

Food	Quantity	Yield
chocolate (bitter)	1 ounce	1 square
coconut	2²/₃ cups	1¹/₂ pounds
marshmallows	16	¹/₂ pound
graham crackers	14 squares	1 cup fine crumbs
vanilla wafers	22	1 cup fine crumbs
bread	1¹/₂ slices	1 cup soft crumbs
bread	1 slice	¹/₂ cup fine, dry crumbs
egg whites	8–10	1 cup
egg yolks	10–12	1 cup
egg (whole)	4–5	1 cup
flavored gelatin	3¹/₂ ounces	¹/₂ cup
unflavored gelatin	¹/₂ ounce	1 tbsp.
nuts (chopped)	1 cup	¹/₂ pound
almonds	3¹/₂ cups	1 pound
walnuts (broken)	3 cups	1 pound
raisins	1 pound	3¹/₂ cups
rice	2¹/₃ cups	1 pound
American Cheese (grated)	5 cups	1 pound
American Cheese (cubed)	2²/₃ cups	1 pound
cream cheese	6²/₃ tbsp.	3-ounce package
zwieback (crumbled)	4	1 cup
banana (mashed)	1 medium	¹/₃ cup
coffee (ground)	5 cups	1 pound
evaporated milk	1 cup	3 cups whipped

References

Bonvie, Linda and Bill, and Gates, Donna, *The Stevia Story - A tale of incredible sweetness and intrigue*, Atlanta: B.E.D. Publications, 1997.

Dufty, William, *Sugar Blues*, New York: Warner Books Inc., 1975.

Ishii, E.L. and Bracht, A., *Glucose release by the liver under conditions of reduced activity of glucose 6-phosphatase*, Laboratorio de Metabolismo Hepatico, Universidade de Maringa, Brasil, July 1987.

Kinghorn, A. Douglas, *Food Ingredient Safety Review: Stevia rebaudiana leaves*, College of Pharmacognosy, University of Illinois at Chicago, March, 1992.

Nakayama, Kunio; Kasahara, Daigo and Yamamoto, Fumihiro, *Absorption, distribution, metabolism and excretion of Stevioside in Rats*, Omiya Research Laboratory, Nikken Chemicals Co. Ltd., Saitama, Japan, March 1985.

Pinheiro, Carlos Eduardo, *Effect of the Stevioside and of the aqueous extract of Stevia Rebaudiana (BERT) Bertoni on the glycemia of normal and diabetic rats*, Presented to the II Brazilian Convention on Stevia Rebaudiana (Bert) Bertoni, September 1982.

Stevia *Rebaudiana: Description and Chemical Aspects*, Inga S.A., Maringa, Brazil, 1989.

Stoddard, Mary Nash, *Deadly Deception - Story of Aspartame*, Dallas: Odenwald Press, 1998.

Stoddard, Mary Nash, *Sweeteners Inspire Bitter Political Battle Between Feds and Consumers*,Nutrition & Healing, June 1998.

Toyoda, K., *Assessment of the carcinogenicity of stevioside in rats*, Food and Chemical Toxicology, June 1997.

Internet References

Aspartame Consumer Safety Network
http://web2.airmail.net/marystod

Herb Research Foundation
http://www.herbs.org

Journalists Linda and Bill Bonvie
http://members.bellatlantic.net

Sugar-Free Cooking With Stevia
http://www.steviapetition.org

Index

Sugar-Free Cooking With Stevia

O

oatmeal, see oats
oats,
    Maple Breakfast Oatmeal, 58
    Oatmeal Wheat Muffins, 53
    Stevia Fruit Smoothie, 43
Oil Pastry, 159
Old Fashion Catsup, 213
Old Fashioned Root Beer (and other soda
    pops), 38
olives,
    Greek Pasta Shrimp Salad, 76
    Pasta Salad, 77
opposition to stevia, 9-10, 21-24
orange juice, see orange
oranges,
    Iced Cappuccino, 36
    Melon Salad, 80
    Orange Cookie Crust, 160
    Orange Frozen Yogurt, 180
    Orange Jubilee, 41
    Orange or Lemon Cream Cheese Glaze, 192
    Orange Sauce, 199
    Orange-Cranberry Sauce, 221
    Orange-Spinach Toss, 79
    Peachy Yogurt Shake, 42
    Poached Pears, 174
    Spiced Cider, 34

P

pancakes,
    Cinnamon-Apple Puffed Oven Pancake, 60
    Pancakes, 59
    Buttermilk Pancakes, 59
    Buckwheat Pancakes, 59
    Nutty Pancakes, 59
papaya,
    Jungle Smoothie, 42
    Stevia Fruit Smoothie, 43
pasta,
    Greek Pasta Shrimp Salad, 76
    Pasta Salad, 77
    Pasta with Tofu, 114
pastries and Crusts,
    Coconut Crust, 161
    Cheese Pastry, 157
    Cookie Crust, 160
    Chocolate Cookie Crust, 160
    Orange Cookie Crust, 160
    Double Crust Pastry, 157
    Grape-Nuts' Crust, 161
    Oil Pastry, 159
    Pretzel Crust, 162

    Rich Pastry, 159
    Single Crust Pastry, 158
peach,
    Freezer Jam, 208
    Peach Butter, 207
    Peach Cobbler, 173
    Peachy Yogurt Shake, 42
    Pineapple-Peach Smoothie, 43
peanut butter,
    Peanut Butter Balls, 184
    Peanut Butter Cookies, 128
pears, see Poached Pears
pecans,
    Chocolate Cake Brownies, 120
    Pecan Sandies, 124
    Sweet Potato Casserole, 95
petition, 229
Picante Sauce, 217
pies,
    Apple Pie, 145
    Banana Cream Pie, 147
    Cherry Pie, 146
    Chocolate Cream Pie, 148
    Coconut Custard Pie, 150
    Key Lime Pie, 152
    Lemon Meringue Pie, 151
    Meringue for Pies, 156
    Nutty Coconut Cream Pie, 149
    Pumpkin Pie, 156
    Sour Cream and Raisin Pie, 155
    Strawberry Chiffon Pie, 154
    Strawberry Cream Cheese Pie, 153
    Vanilla Cream Pie, 147
Pina Colada Frozen Yogurt, 181
pineapple
    Jungle Smoothie, 42
    Pina Colada Frozen Yogurt, 181
    Pineapple Chicken, 101
    Pineapple Upside-Down Cake, 134
    Pineapple-Peach Smoothie, 43
    Sweet & Sour Chicken, 102
    Sweet and Sour Carrots, 90
Pinheiro, Carlos Eduardo, 7
Poached Pears, 174
Poppy Seed Dressing, 82
potatoes,
    Corn Chowder, 65
    German-Style Potato Salad, 72
powder form, 8, 14-15
Powdered Sugar Substitute, 188
preserves,
    Apple Butter, 206
    Freezer Jam, 208
    Fruit Juice Jelly, 209
    Peach Butter, 207

Visit the web site of Crystal Health Publishing for
upcoming book information, and the latest news about

Sugar-Free Cooking With Stevia

http://www.steviapetition.org

Order additional copies of *Cooking with Stevia* on-line at our web site,
or by writing to the address below.

EDUCATIONAL AND GROUP DISCOUNTS AVAILABLE.
FOR MORE INFORMATION WRITE TO:

Crystal Health Publishing
PO Box 171683
Arlington, Texas 76017